Miniature Antiques

By the same author

Dolls' Houses

The Pleasure of Your Company
A HISTORY OF MANNERS AND MEALS

Top: Purse with miniature views of Paris; blue glass scent-bottle, silver top and ring for carrying; small purse framed in tortoiseshell with Italian view (all nineteenth century); enamel acorn spice box continental c 1690.

Middle: Eighteenth century straw-work French love-token box; early eighteenth century silver counter-box; French (Paris) snuff-box of ivory mounted in gilt, set with a miniature portrait of Mother and Child painted in gouache on mother-of-pearl, box lined with tortoiseshell c 1775-81; silver cartouche-shaped vinaigrette by John Shaw, 1790; Scottish snuff-box of varnished wood with coaching scene, early nineteenth century; mother-of-pearl fish toothpick; German pocket terrestrial globe.

Bottom: Miniature almanack for 1792 in tooled-leather binding and slip-case; bead decorated needlecase; straw-work needlecase in slip-case, early nineteenth century.

Photo by Studio Wreford

Collecting
Miniature Antiques

JEAN LATHAM

WITH 4 COLOR PLATES
AND 67 BLACK AND WHITE PHOTOGRAPHS

Charles Scribner's Sons
New York

c1972

Contents

	PAGE
INTRODUCTION	9
Miniature Books	11
Miniature Brass	22
Buttons and Shoe Buckles	30
Miniature Clothes	40
Miniature Curiosities	49
Dolls	55
Fans	68
Miniature Furniture	75
Miniature Glass	87
Miniature Jewellery and Small Boxes	92
Miniature Portraits	105
Miniature Pottery and Porcelain	119
Rings	133
Miniature Silver	140
Toys	150
Looking After Your Collection	169
BIBLIOGRAPHY	177

Illustrations

COLOR

A collection of miniature antiques   *Frontispiece*

FACING PAGE

Eighteenth century crèche figure clothes   49
A collection of 19th century dolls   64
Miniature Dolls' House   160

BLACK AND WHITE

PAGE

Paper Doll book called 'The History of Little Fanny'   17
The 'Boarding-School Romps'—an example of a Harlequinade   19
Regency fire place with chimney ornaments   25
Two copper kettles and a brass coffee pot   26
Two brass paper weights and a duck paper clip   27
A late 17th century brass and copper dog-collar   28
French buttons, dated 1870   34
French 18th century buttons of 'Monuments of Paris'   35
Set of six different 18th century French steel buttons, *c.* 1795   36
Set of four seasons on porcelain   36
Metal Art Nouveau button   37
18th century button from a set of the Italian Comedy   37
18th century clothes for crèche figures   42
A cream-coloured fine wool dress for an adult doll   43
Doll's corset, *c.* 1850   45
A selection of doll's shoes, boots, gloves and accessories   47
Unusual oriental silver-mounted pumice-stone   52
A stirrup jug in the form of a hound and two miniature glass
  boots for stirrup cups.   53
Minton joke-mug, mid-19th century   53
Early 19th century workbox in the form of a house   54
An 18th century barber's powder-bellows with the glassmaker's
  example used for toilet-water   54
Crèche figure in original clothes, probably late 18th century from
  Italy   56
The baby cries and kicks his legs as the carriage moves   58
A collection of 19th century dolls   60
A Jumeau doll with bisque head and arms   61
Late 18th century automata, playing the mandolin   62
A French fan, 1860–70 with guards and sticks of carved ivory
by Brisevi   69

	PAGE
Beautiful Italian fan, *c.* 1700	70
An Italian fan, *c.* 1750	71
An English fan, *c.* 1800	74
18th century miniature furniture	78
Two sample chairs	79
Doll's chair of the Second Empire period	79
A French 18th century toilet-table for dolls	80
19th century miniature glass	82
A dinner-table centrepiece made at Nevers	83
Nevers spun-glass crèche	84
Three miniature glass candle sticks	87
Two lace or tie pins	96
Pendant-brooch, *c.* 1860–80	97
A beautiful miniature signed by John Smart and dated 1776	106
Water colour by Peter Oliver	107
A miniature of a gentleman by Richmond Cosway	109
A charming miniature of Mary Louisa Inglis by George Engleheart	110
A large circular Games Box by Raven	112
Portrait inscribed Mlle. H. Sonntag on a Stobwasser box	113
George IV painted *after Lawrence* on a Stobwasser box	113
16th century wax portraits	118
Doll's dinner service in Staffordshire blue-and-white china	120
Doll's food; Plaster painted in bright colours	122
A pair of 'image toys' made in Staffordshire *c.* 1850	123
Staffordshire pottery cradle of Napoleon's, unfortunate son *Le Roi de Rome*	123
A collection of 19th century German China fairings	125
Model of a booth at a fair, Staffordshire, about 1830	125
Four nineteenth century rings	137
Miniature teapot, coffee pot, and cream jug, en suite, mid-19th century	141
Rare cornucopia posy holder by Joseph Willmore	143
A Victorian silver chatelaine hall-marked and dated 1877	144
A mid-19th century horse and cart	152
Miniature doll's house	156
Fishmonger's shop (*c.* 1840)	157
Typical Amsterdam town house	158
An example of a dissected puzzle	161
18th century cards found in a notary's client's files	165

Acknowledgements

First, my grateful thanks to the Director and the Editor of *Collectors Guide* for permission to quote passages, where relevant, from articles which I wrote for them; also for allowing me to use some of the photographs I used to illustrate those articles. I should like to thank Monsieur Victor Houart who so kindly allowed me to reproduce photographs from his collection of rare buttons; I particularly want to thank Mr Rupert Gentle for his kindness in letting me reproduce many photographs of his stock of beautiful treasures; and I am grateful to Miss Celia Haynes and family for the illustration of their Dutch dolls' house and to Studio Wreford, Marlborough, for their photography.

Thanks as well to the following bodies for giving me permission to use photographs from their collections:– The Victoria and Albert Museum; Messrs. Sotheby & Co.; The Trustees of the Wallace Collection; The Trustees of the London Museum; The Art Gallery and Museum, High Wycombe; The Syndics of the Fitzwilliam Museum, Cambridge; The Musée des Arts et Métiers, The Musée d'Histoire de l'Education and The Musée des Arts Décoratifs, Paris.

Introduction

Before embarking on a discussion of miniature antiques, it is just as well to define the word miniature and to decide how we intend to use it. As Humpty Dumpty said to Alice, 'When *I* use a word it means just what I choose it to mean—neither more nor less.' To which Alice replied very sensibly, 'The question is whether you *can* make words mean so many different things.'

Miniature comes from the past participle, *miniato*, of the Italian verb *miniare*, to dye, paint or colour with red lead or vermilion. In Latin *minium* refers to red lead or cinnabar and is said by Skeat to be Spanish in origin. Our word miniature or small painting is *miniatura* in Italian. The first letters of early illuminated manuscripts were usually designed in red and gold and often had a small picture painted in vermilion or red lead and gold leaf inside the letter.

Here then is the derivation of the word miniature, but nowadays any very small object is described in this term. For the purposes of our book we will be very elastic over its meaning and include not only true miniatures, pictures, portraits, and small replicas of things that are generally big like furniture and even houses; but also we will talk about diminutive objects like buttons, thimbles and 'toys' both in its present-day sense and in its 18th century use, meaning trifles that amuse adults. In old Dutch the word *tuyg*, pronounced like toy with a g on the end, meant what we call a chatelaine, those useful chased hooks that carried scissors, watch, vinaigrette and other necessities at the end of long chains and were attached to a lady's belt in the middle ages. From about 1837 to 1860, following this cult for reviving medieval fashions, chatelaines were very popular. They only finally lost favour at the end of the century.

Practically everything we use has been made in diminished size. There is an immediate appeal in smaller-than-life objects, which the psychologists might perhaps explain as a search for lost childhood. Certainly very few of us can resist the lure of a well-stocked toyshop window, or those magical shops in the Burlington Arcade filled with exquisite antique brooches, buckles, rings and other ornaments, tiny and infinitely desirable, in fact what the 18th century people called 'toys'.

When planning a picture, a lecture, a book, several choices lie open to us, and like Jane Austen's *Emma*, when she intended to read more, we may probably make out lists 'very well chosen and very neatly arranged—sometimes alphabetically and sometimes by some other rule.' In the case of miniature antiques, so numerous and varied and so enchanting, we will look at them chiefly grouped in their different materials, glass, wood, silver, brass and so forth, but classifying a few under such headings as Toys, Houses and, the easy way out for all the odds and ends, under Miscellaneous.

The following small treasures, to be found in all sorts of unlikely shops, markets, attics and old people's untidy drawers, are some of great worth and some of little value. But they have one thing in common and that is the desirable quality of evoking the past and stirring our imaginations.

MINIATURE BOOKS

I

True Miniature Books

Originally designed to fit conveniently into the pockets of 17th and 18th century gentlemen or into those delightful ladies' pockets worn tied round the waist between dress and petticoats, the first miniature books were made in this minute size to enable people to carry about with them easily a bible, a prayer-book or a book of poems. As coat-pockets were not invented until the 17th century some sort of receptacle for carrying things like pomanders or snuff-boxes, money, handkerchiefs and so forth was a necessity. The mediaeval people had no such convenience as a pocket, but in the 16th century pockets in trunk hose and later in breeches appeared. There was a useful double-pocket, exactly like some of our kitchen and garden aprons of today, that came into use for for market women in the 18th century, and mediaeval women carried purses hung round their waists.

However, as far as books were concerned only very small ones could be carried about, obviously. Later on came a vogue for these very tiny publications, just for the sake of their microscopic size, and the skill in setting up this miniscule type was remarkable. One of the greatest authorities on miniature books, Mr. Percy Edwin Spielmann, has over 500 of these little gems of exquisite production in his collection and the smallest is less than a quarter of an inch high. His catalogue itself is a collector's piece and all collectors refer to it for classifying their own works.

Modern miniature books are still in production. Approximate sizes are mostly from $3\frac{3}{4}$ by $2\frac{1}{4}$ inches, $2\frac{1}{2}$ by $1\frac{7}{8}$ inches, and $1\frac{7}{8}$ by $1\frac{1}{4}$ inches. So beautifully printed in a special non-clogging ink on prepared paper, these small works of art can be read quite easily with spectacles. Sometimes volumes, especially the little bibles, have a small magnifying glass included in a pocket.

Mr. Spielmann's collection is limited to volumes no more than 3 inches high, including some remarkable manuscript books, such as a *Book of the Hours* circa 1500, which is illuminated.

There are even miniature book-plates, though these are rarities. Mr. Spielmann's collection has a specially designed book-plate in two sizes.

Another collector of great importance is Mr. Louis W. Bondy. His bookshop too is a treasure-house for bibliophiles and the discovery of one of his sales catalogues about 15 years ago led me into the search for miniature almanacs and for childrens' books, which we will discuss briefly later on.

In 1784 over 380,000 almanacs were sold by the Company of Stationers. In 1773 a courageous publisher called Thomas Carnan, defied the Company, which had hitherto enjoyed a monopoly, granted to them in 1603, of printing these very popular almanacs. He did not win his case until 1779, but when he did he printed in his next almanac a statement to honour his successful petition.

One of the entertaining bonuses from collecting almanacs is the amusing entries about events of the day. For instance, 'Three comets' appeared in 1662 and '2 Whales in the Thames' in 1669. Another almanac noted some 'Remarkable Events' of past years in which was included 'Noah's Flood, Ann. Ant. Christum 2348'; this entry is appropriately followed by, 'Tide so high at Westminster that the lawyers were fetched out of the hall in boats. 24 March, 1734.' A beautifully bound almanac in red morocco decorated in gold and blue and with a matching slip-case, is printed in black and red and has weather forecasts. It is compiled by John Goldsmith and printed by the Company of Stationers, dated 1792, 'being Bissextile or LEAP-YEAR.' One of the 'Remarkable Events' chronicled is 'Creation of the World, Ann. Ant. Christum, 23 Oct. 4004.' Much later Strange's *Victoria Miniature Almanack* for 1851 noted the 'First Hippopotamus into England.'

Besides these gay little entries there are more serious references to weather, lunar and solar cycles, money tables, dictionaries of dates, days of Fairs and information about distinguished public servants.

Collectors should remember that the London almanacs were engraved until 1874, consequently the scenes included of London are very beautiful. When, after 1874, they were printed from type, the result was a noticeable coarsening in the pictures. In 1894 and 1895, Spielmann tells us, the half-tone blocks, which were made from photographs, bring the standard down further.

The bindings of these delightful little books are as varied as jewels. Besides ordinary paper reinforced, they are bound in leather, sharkskin, velvet and sycamore wood, and also they are exquisitely bound in mother-of-pearl, tortoiseshell, bone, pinchbeck, silver and even gold. I have an example of a gold case, with the almanac inside it intact; the monogram initials are surmounted by a coronet and the legend beneath reads 'Ob. 17th Nov. 1818'. This gold case may have been a memorial.

Spielmann mentions one of black tortoiseshell with a lock of hair inside the top cover under glass mounted in gold. This almanac's case is engraved with a girl's name, her age and the date, '5th Oct. 1824'. The almanac, however, is *The London Almanack for 1825. Printed for the Company of Stationers.* It has the tax stamp in red on the inner page, which cost the publisher 1s. 3d. for each almanac in 1829, this tax eventually being removed in 1834.

My favourite almanac is for 1836. It is a tiny object with gilded pages, only $1\frac{1}{8}$ inches by $\frac{3}{4}$ of an inch in size. It is bound in brilliant emerald green in thick paper and has a golden rose stamped on the little slipcase. The condition is nearly perfect, with only a small tear on the case. The frontispiece reads, '*The English Bijou Almanac for 1836, poetically illustrated by L.E.L. LONDON. Schloss, 2 Gt. Russell Street.*' In Spielmann's catalogue his 1838 almanac of this series is published by 'Schloss, 42 Gt. Russell Street, London', which appeared to be a very slight variation on mine. The L.E.L. refers to the poetess Letitia Elizabeth Landon (1802–1838), who has written the poetic tributes beside the engraved portraits of Hemans and Raffaelle, amongst others. A tiny piece of green silk ribbon marks the place for the reader, and an early page has a miniature laurel wreath delicately etched, with the words 'Presented to . . .' printed inside it. For safety this unbelievably small book, so clearly readable through a glass, lies in the basket of my (circa 1830) pedlar girl. She also carries a minute song-sheet called *Le Troubadour*, which belongs to her originally and in fact, for the record, *The English Bijou Almanac* is the only object on her tray which is not her own. Mr. Louis Bondy, in his *Miniature Books Catalogue* No. 69, points out that this series is 'one of the miracles of miniature book production' and he mentions that the publisher Schloss dedicated the 1837 almanac to Queen Victoria. Spielmann's catalogue specially remarks upon the almost unbelievably fine engraving of the four pages of music which end this 1837 Almanac.

French almanacs of this tiny size are rare. It is worth hunting for the publisher Marcilly's tiny miniscule series which first appeared in 1798, ending in 1849. The 1803 almanac 'Le Joujou Amusant' has twelve engraved plates, mostly of children playing, and the size is $1\frac{3}{16}$ inches by $\frac{13}{16}$ of an inch. Foreign almanacs also came from Austria, Belgium, Czechoslovakia, Denmark, Germany, Holland and Italy.

The Miniature History of England, with a frontispiece showing the Houses of Parliament, published circa 1903 by Goode Bros., is another charming little production. My own copy, alas, has the cover repaired, but the portraits and information about the English sovereigns from William the Conqueror to Edward VII are in excellent condition and the clearness of the print is remarkable. There is also a later edition ending with George V, dated circa 1910. Both tiny volumes are $1\frac{3}{8}$ inches by $1\frac{1}{8}$ inches. The very smallest books of all are $\frac{3}{16}$ of an inch square.

Kate Greenaway's almanacs are one of the few miniature books well known to non-collectors. They were published from 1883 to 1895 and then again in 1897, by George Routledge and Sons and there are several variants in the bindings. They are very appealing little books and used to cost a shilling apiece. *Kate Greenaway's Alphabet*, by the same publisher is another charming book, measuring $2\frac{5}{8}$ inches by $2\frac{3}{8}$ inches. The Empress Eugénie had an enormous collection of miniature books amounting, it is said, to several thousand, but alas they were destroyed or at any rate disappeared at the time of the Commune. Another royal lady, Queen Mary, was presented with a large library of tiny books in the famous dolls' house designed by Sir Edwin Lutyens and now at Windsor Castle. Her books were described and catalogued in *The Library of the Queen's Dolls' House*, edited by E. V. Lucas. Besides the almanacs we have already described *The English Bijou Almanac* and one *London Almanack* (for 1833), there are diminutive atlases and dictionaries, histories, Bibles and Shakespeare and

French books of the early 19th century, as well as *Whitaker*, *Who's Who*, A.B.C. railway guides, and copies of magazines and newspapers.

II
Small Children's Books

The fascinating realm of children's books are divided into two categories. There are the little books written purely for entertainment, and the others intended for instruction, in which we include religion. Foreign books equally fit into these classifications.

John Harris (1756–1846) is a publisher who was particularly associated with both kinds of children's books, carrying on the business of another famous publisher John Newbery (1713–1767) after his death. In 1745 Newbery not only published but also wrote children's books and indeed he was a pioneer in this field. When he died his son took over his business and subsequently Harris joined him. In those days publishers often went in for sidelines to increase their incomes and whilst Newbery sold patent medicines, Harris manufactured and sold indelible marking ink. Harris's churchyard address appears at least as early as 1802; and earlier, in 1744, Newbery opened his business in Temple Bar, London. His *Little Pretty Pocket-Book* was recently reprinted in facsimile. Apparently the book originally cost 6d. alone, while accompanied by 'a Ball or a Pincushion' the price was 8d. 'Pretty' seems to have been an adjective much in favour, as many others amongst Newbery's children's book were called 'Pretty' this or that. Incidentally he was quite uneducated but an astute businessman, enterprising, honest and ambitious. Most of his thirty-five or so children's books were educational in their subjects, such as *Alphabet Royal* (1750), *Spelling Dictionary* (1755), *Wonders of Art and Nature* (1758) and others.

When John Harris, who had been Elizabeth Newbery's manager for years, finally took over the business in the early 19th century he had an outstanding success with his juvenile publications, which were embellished with metal engravings gaily hand-coloured. Besides the famous Old Mother Hubbard stories published in 1805 and illustrated with engravings of Sarah Catherine Martin's drawings, Harris is probably best known for *The Butterfly's Ball and the Grasshopper's Feast*. Copies of this little book might be bought plain or coloured. It appeared on January 1st, 1807, the author being at once an M.P., a banker and a retired attorney, called William Roscoe. He had written the poems for his small son. The success of this book was followed by *The Peacock 'At Home'*, by A Lady (Mrs. Dorset), which had been commissioned by Harris. No less than 40,000 copies were sold in one year and now more and more children could have the pleasure of being amused and not only instructed in their books.

In 1823 came a delightful book, which has been re-published in facsimile, called *Dame Wiggins of Lea, and her seven wonderful cats*. The re-issue is late Victorian, but so popular was it that another edition may well have been produced since then. This book also is a small size, and the early spelling books and reading books are mostly in our category of miniatures too.

One of the most enchanting groups is the series of paper-doll books, published by S. & J. Fuller between 1810 and 1812. The most famous were *The History and Adventures of Little Henry* (1810), *The History of Little Fanny* (1811), *Ellen, or the Naughty Girl Reclaimed* (1811), *Phoebe, the Cottage Maid* (1811), and best of all, *Cinderella, or the Little Glass Slipper* (1814). They all were published with a board case to match the cover, with a silk ribbon to tie across the top and keep safe the cut-out figures in each book of poems which were hand-coloured and provided with different heads and hats. They are rarely found intact, but I once found *Little Fanny* with nothing missing. (See illustration.) These books were very expensive by standards of the day, costing between five and eight shillings (25–40p). Of course comparing past prices with those of today is not very rewarding, as it depends upon how much a shilling would buy in the days under discussion. Nowadays they could fetch at least £50 apiece.

Coming into our present century we have the incomparable Beatrix Potter, whose *Peter Rabbit* appeared in print in 1901, although his story was completed some time before this date. Miss Lane's biography of the author states that *Peter Rabbit*'s adventures had first been told in a letter, for the benefit of a sick boy of five years old, in 1893. This classic series of animal stories has never since been out of print with those charming pictures by the author. Surely they will take their place amongst the immortal children's books.

The hat and clothes slip on to the figure in this Paper Doll book called 'The History of Little Fanny, exemplified in a series of figures' published by S. & J. Fuller in 1810.

One very rare and most entertaining type of book is called a Harlequinade. About 1760, or a little before, a print-shop in Fleet Street was taken over by Robert Sayer. It was an important business and Sayer brought with him a new idea invented by himself, which continued to be popular for about thirty years. When this small oblong paperback is opened it reveals pictures, which are cut in half at the centre. They are folded back in turn to show the verses that tell the story of each picture. Every verse ends by instructing the reader to turn down the next flap so that the new picture which is disclosed fits into position. First called 'turn-ups', or 'metamorphoses', these dramatic little stories were later christened 'Harlequinades', when Sayer had yet another good idea. He decided to make each 'turn-up' book tell the story of a current pantomime or harlequinade that was then showing in London. Other publishers followed suit, amongst them the enterprising Harris. T. Hughes seems to have been the chief rival to Sayer, however.[1]

Mr. Percy Muir writes most interestingly about these unusual small books in his classic, *English Children's Books*. He has traced their origin to a 'parlour pastime' of the 17th century or even earlier. He knows no printed examples earlier than those of Robert Sayer, but he reproduces a manuscript example which he dates circa 1698.

My own specimen is called *The Boarding-School Romps*, and seems rather more suitable for adults than for children. It does not appear in Mr. Muir's list of the ones published by Robert Sayer, nor in the list of 'Other Publishers'. It was in fact published on June 18th, 1771, by 'William Tringham and others' and was to be found at 'most of ye Booksellers, Stationers and Toy Shops of Great Britain and Ireland' (see illustration). There is a coloured example at the Museum of Childhood in Edinburgh. Until 1835, it is worth remembering, coloured illustrations were always done by hand, and generally the coloured editions were small. Probably a certain number of the more numerous uncoloured editions were coloured at home, as some of them are very carelessly done indeed. Many early children's books seem very rough and ready to us now, but remember that the publishers had to keep their prices

[1] Percy Muir's *English Children's Books*. Pub. B. T. Batsford Ltd. 1953.

THE BOARDING SCHOOL
R O M P S.
Obferve the Fathers cautious Air,
While Colombine is void of Care,
He thinks her wildnefs much to blame
And Seeks a place to Make her Tame:
While he his Romping Daughter leads,
Turn up, and find if he Succeeds.

The Father's in a mighty rage,
She Kneels his Pafsion to Afsuage;
He threatens hard, She begs, & Prays,
And he relents at what She Says;
Turn Down, & you'll the Sequel find,
That Love to Conftancy is kind.

Tringham Jun.r Invent et Sculp.t
London, Publish'd June 13.th 1771. as ÿ Act directs,
by Wm Tringham, under St Dunftans Church,
Fleet Street; Henry Wafs, Lad Lane; L. Merry, next ÿ
London Tavern, Bishopsgate Street; J. Tomlinson, White
Chapel; Wm Harris, St Pauls Church Yard; & most
of ÿ Bookfellers, Stationers & Toy Shops of
Great Britain & Ireland.
Price Six Pence. Coloured 1 Shilling.

The 'Boarding-School Romps' is an example of a
Harlequinade. Published on June 13th, 1771, by
Wm. Tringham and others, it sold for sixpence (one
shilling coloured) and was found at 'most of ye Book-
sellers, Stationers and Toy Shops of Great Britain and
Ireland'. It is very rare.

low and the editions small, which of course is why they are so rare today. Another problem for the early publishers was that until machines replaced handwork for the setting of the type, binding the books together, the paper-making, printing and colouring the more expensive editions, the process of book production was slow and laborious and quite expensive, in spite of the cheap labour and materials. Mr. Muir points out that the price of children's books in the early 19th century was hardly any cheaper than in the 1950's. The hand-colouring for the publishers was often farmed out to families, with the children doing most of the work.

In the 1830's George Baxter began to produce the prints that are so much collected today, and although at first the new process was too expensive for children's books, by the 1850's it was sufficiently cheap to produce coloured frontispieces for them. The process was far less meticulously done by the Kronheims, so that by the 1860's rather crude and garish pictures appeared in children's books, which certainly compare very unfavourably with the hand-coloured ones.

Another interesting aspect of children's book illustrations is the fact that from the 1860's publishers were bidding for sales of juvenilia by employing first-class artists like Millais, Tenniel, Arthur Hughes, Keene and Birket Foster. This led on to Walter Crane, Caldecott and Kate Greenaway illustrations, which are all particularly successful and sought after by collectors.

Walter Crane's magnificent colour and design is exceptional. Over-elaborate it may be, but the richness of his artistic imagination and colouring seem to fit the texts remarkably well. His first series of 'sixpenny toy-books' appeared in 1866, using here only black, red and blue. Kate Greenaway and Caldecott are considered even better illustrators than Crane by many people and the small books of Kate Greenaway are amongst the most popular that are collected today.

Caldecott's toy books appeared first in 1878, according to Mr. Percy Muir, who gives a list from unpublished notes of the colour-printer Edmund Evans. They were published by Routledge.

Richard Doyle of *Punch*, George Cruikshank, Gordon Browne, son of the celebrated 'Phiz', Arthur Rackham and legions of other illustrators were pressed into the field of children's books to the great benefit of children past and present.

20

When we consider that the 1930 catalogue issued in Paris by Gumuchian and Co., had over 6,000 entries, it is not surprising if this short resumé of even the tiny sized books is incomplete and only skims the surface. Those interested in exploring the subject further will find suggestions for reading at the end of this book. Nor must it be forgotten that there were also innumerable books in other languages equally attractive and desirable.

MINIATURE BRASS

I

Alloys of Copper

An alloy of copper and zinc, brass is that lovely golden coloured metal that the Elizabethans used to call latten and it was invented many thousands of years ago. It is not as ancient as bronze, another alloy which is composed of copper with varying amounts of tin. Bronze was in use from about 2500 B.C.

There are a great number of other alloys of copper which have been used by metal workers throughout history. For instance an alloy of copper, zinc and nickel has been used for electro-plating from about 1840, which was either called Nickel Silver or German Silver and this is what was eventually stamped with the letters E.P.N.S., meaning of course electro plated nickel silver. It was originally called argentan and replaced copper as a base for plating silver; collectors of Sheffield plate always bear in mind the date 1840 as the end of their best period. Another silver substitute was Britannia Metal, first of all named white metal and invented in the last half of the 18th century, and this also was an alloy of copper mixed with a very little tin and some antimony. There is another alloy called Dutch metal which looks like brass and was used for gilding picture frames more cheaply than using gold leaf.

Ormolu of course is very well known, particularly in France where bronze, finished with a covering of gold is called *bronze dorée* and much used for china and furniture mounts. The famous Matthew Boulton, a silversmith of the 18th century working in Birmingham made ormolu mounts of excellent quality.

One of the best known alloys was Pinchbeck, called after its inventor, a watchmaker. Christopher Pinchbeck died in 1732 and his son Edward popularized the metal, but he appears, like his Father, to have kept the secret of this zinc and copper alloy's exact mixture, describing its resemblance to gold 'in colour, smell and ductility' and adding that he would not dispose of 'one grain of this curious metal' to anybody else.

An alloy that resists tarnish, looking like silver, was made from nickel, zinc and copper in China and imported over here during the 18th century to make grates and fenders, besides candlesticks and other pieces. This was called Paktong. A mysterious nutmeg grater came into my possession which I would like to think was an example of this unusual metal; but except that it appears to date to circa 1820, according to the researches I have made, and that it certainly resists tarnish, I have not yet verified its attributions. Of course the alloy called steel or speculum, which was used for making ancient hand mirrors, takes a high polish so that it looks like silver too. There is an interesting collection of steel mirrors in the Louvre.

The last alloy worth mentioning here, though there are countless others, is the brass-like metal invented by Prince Rupert of the Rhine, son of the beautiful Elizabeth of Bohemia and nephew of Charles I. This type of brass is called Prince's metal and how exciting it would be to find buttons made of it. Geoffrey Wills' most interesting book on collecting copper and brass notes that the first Earl of Bristol, John Hervey, wrote in his diary for January 1690 that he had paid £1. 10s. for 'six dozen of Princes metal buttons'.[1]

II

Small Brass Treasures

There are so many attractive little pieces of brass to be found that it is quite difficult to know where to begin or where to end. Perhaps the wisest way for a collector to take is to start by acquiring pieces from an expert dealer. Poor finish on modern reproductions gives them away, and a join showing as a raised line is suspect, even when ground away in order to deceive the unwary: for this means a mould of the original article has been made and when removed from the two sides of the mould the piece retains this tell-tale ridge. Horse brasses are not for the beginner either, nor candlesticks, many of which have been copied frequently. Once you have acquired some genuine old brass, however, it is easy to compare purchases with your best pieces and this advice is worth

[1]*Collecting Copper & Brass.* Geoffrey Wills, 1962.

following in all branches of antique collecting. It is extraordinary how immediate the impact of a modern reproduction is when placed amongst the true antiques. The new piece invariably stands out like a sore thumb, unless it is an exceptionally fine piece of deception. Then you may as well keep it for your rogue's gallery. Some fakes become respectable with age.

Probably our subject of miniatures is where the forger has not been at work. The little brass objects like dolls' house fire-irons, fenders, trivets and chandeliers were too fiddling and not sufficiently rewarding financially for the forgers' attention. There are many delightfully small brass fireplaces, probably samples to be taken round by craftsmen to display their range of work, and some are complete with fenders and fire-irons. You may find tiny fenders with brass lion's paws for feet, probably early 19th century. The fire-irons are also of this date, as in the 18th century sets were generally made from steel. The fenders of the 18th century were often of brass and much lower than Victorian ones. Small, or for that matter large kettles are mostly 19th century and the kettles on stands are late 19th century.

Smokers' toys made from brass are legion. The pipes were even occasionally made of cast brass in England during the 18th century, but they can have hardly been very pleasant to smoke as brass certainly holds the heat. There were, however, silver pipes in the early days of smoking and probably this was when the less affluent smoker had to settle for brass.

Pipe-stoppers in many shapes, besides the ubiquitous legs and arms, can be found quite easily. The handle ends show animals' heads, birds, dogs and even fishes, as well as characters like Nelson or Britannia, Punch, Ally Sloper, figures from Dickens' novels, famous highwaymen, sportsmen or even the Pope himself.

Brass tobacco boxes and snuff-boxes are desirable, with scenes stamped or engraved on them, and once I saw a beautiful brass box with the punched holes of a cribbage board on its lid.

The writing table also offers many charming brass articles, particularly for holding letters or papers together. Paper weights made of brass appear as hands, mostly in Queen Victoria's reign, and also paper-clips with the registration diamond mark stamped on the cuff or elsewhere, so that you may actually date your find to the very day of the month, as well as the year, in which it was

Regency fire place with chimney ornaments; presumably this is a trade sample from Scotland to judge by the outsize thistle.

made. Brass seals are in several forms and one in my possession is a cube like a dice with portraits on each side. Prince Albert, Queen Victoria, Wellington and even Shakespeare and Oliver Cromwell are amonst them. One of my favourite seals is a wheel with mottoes on each of the six hubs. One is inscribed forget-me-not, with the flower; another is the Duke of Wellington on horseback, a third is a hand saying 'ever true'. There are many variants of these seals, but they more often are found with a metal handle when the seals are of semi-precious stones. These are more desirable, perhaps, but do not belong in this chapter strictly speaking. Whist markers with a movable hand, appear in brass and so do cigar-cutters. A penny-farthing bicycle is one example.

An interesting collection can be formed of brass spoons, which were being made in England back in the 16th century. The pewterers, however, were reluctant to have rivals in their line of tablewares, so it is not until the 17th century that collectors can expect to find brass spoons. Their shapes, not surprisingly, tend to copy silver ones of their period. Later they were dipped in tin to resemble silver, which seems sacrilege to lovers of the beautiful metal brass. Forks are more or less unobtainable in brass, chiefly

Two copper kettles and a brass coffee pot (the largest is five inches high).

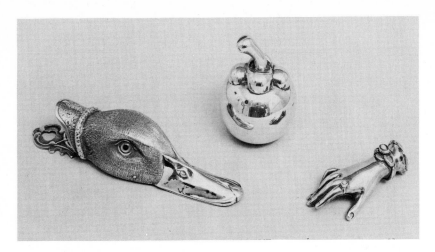

Two brass paper weights and a duck paper clip, all exceptionally good heavy quality as we should expect from the Victorian period.

because in any case forks did not come into general use in Europe, far less in England, until the 17th century. Even as late as the early 19th century many people did not know how to use them, it seems. The early two-pronged forks were mostly used for carving or for serving such delicacies as ginger or preserved fruits. Nobody except the Italians, who used forks in the 16th century, seems to have bothered about the dirty fingers of diners all plunging into the dishes. People are more squeamish nowadays.

A few months ago a most exciting find came my way. It was a small work of art from the late 17th century in the shape of a magnificent brass dog-collar, engraved and pierced and backed with copper.

As usual, at least half the pleasure of discovering an antique is finding out where it came from, who made it and what indeed it was used for. After consulting with an expert at the Victoria and Albert Museum I found an article written in 1933 by Charles R. Beard. In it, to my joy and amazement, he not only referred to my dog-collar, but there were two excellent photographs of it. Apparently the initials A.V.O. surmounted by a coronet, belonged to Aubrey de Vere (1626–1703), the 20th and last Earl of Oxford

A late 17th century brass and copper dog-collar showing a coppersmith's forge. The initials (other side) AVO with coronet are probably those of Aubrey de Vere, Earl of Oxford, who employed many Dutch workers at Castle Hedingham. This collar is of Dutch workmanship.

of the first creation. Mr. Beard cannot be altogether categorical over this attribution as the collar appears to be of Dutch workmanship. But the probability is so great as to seem nearly certain when we find that there was a factory at Wandsworth staffed by Dutchmen at this period and moreover the collar was originally found in Essex at a spot not far from the stronghold belonging to the de Vere family which was called Castle Hedingham.

One specially interesting fact about this collar is that there is a panel on it which shows the inside of a contemporary copper-smith's forge. Having never before seen an ancient dog-collar, very similar, by the way, to those worn by slaves, it was a remarkable stroke of luck to find another later example in brass a few weeks later. This one, probably very early 19th century, bore the legend, 'I am John Rutter's dog of Devizes. Whose dog are you?' This was directly cribbed from the famous collar given to Frederick Prince of Wales, by Alexander Pope and inscribed:

'I am his Highness' dog at Kew,
Pray tell me, Sir, whose dog are you?'

This seems a fitting climax to a chapter about small brass objects.

BUTTONS AND SHOE BUCKLES

I

Buttons

So familiar are these useful little attachments to our clothes that the average person would be unlikely to give a thought to their history. As we button up our overcoats it is interesting to know what an immensely long time they have been in use, either as ornaments or fasteners. In fact they did start out as ornaments, though the origin of them is lost in the mists of antiquity. Henry VIII's portraits show how handsomely they decorated his sumptuous garments, which the costers 'pearly clothes' recall.

It was not until the late 15th century that buttons started their useful lives in Europe, teamed up with buttonholes. In England we only began to secure our clothes with them in the second half of the 16th century.

In their ornamental days buttons were made out of silk or lace and rich men wore them decorated with pearls or made out of 'chrystall', diamonds or rubies, and also of gold and silver. The ones of precious metal were often given designs in relief and the rather ghoulish fashion of the 16th century was to wear buttons in the shape of a skull staring emptily from your sleeve or bosom. Watches and rings were also given this depressing form at this period, just to remind the wearer of the transience of life. This certainly argued a great robustness of temperament in our ancestors. Owing to the weight of silver cast buttons in the early 18th century, noblemen preferred to wear buttons covered with some material like velvet or silk; but this did not last long, for by 1750 fashion decreed that silver, gold or metal ones should be worn. These were usually fitted on to the top of a bone or wooden mould, which was punched with holes through which a thread of cat-gut was pulled and this fastened them to the coat. Metal buttons, precious and semi-precious, would grace military uniforms and also the

30

liveries of servants belonging to stately households.

Round about 1770 the bone or wooden bases of the buttons gradually were replaced by an underplate of silver or silver-gilt fitted with a shank. Of course the livery buttons would have had crests or cyphers engraved on them, whilst the fashionable man-about-town had a very wide choice of motifs.

After the 18th century silver or gilded buttons were hardly made at all because of the cheaper brass and plated ones that competed with them. Crested buttons for servants' liveries were made in several sizes in Sheffield plate between 1760 and 1840.

The forerunner of our postman was the letter-carrier. He was provided with an official uniform in 1793 and the brass buttons on his red tail-coat, with its blue lapels and cuffs, were engraved with the number assigned to the wearer. A little earlier in 1757 the Duke of Bedford spent nearly £5 each on his postilion's suits of velvet and gold braid which were decorated with innumerable gilt buttons.

Enamel hunting and sporting buttons, and those of silver, steel, gilt and brass, were always popular, particularly in the 1750's and 60's. They were embellished with miniature pictures of a fox, a horse, a dog or a pheasant and even a fighting cock or a boar. They are frequently in sets. For example there was a magnificent life-story of a stag designed in gold inlay of different colours on a polished steel body. The workmanship on the buttons looks quite remarkable. Since the vogue for sporting buttons continued well into the 19th century, and Dickens himself wrote an article about them in a magazine called *Household Words*, it would be a very good line for a collector to choose.

The special insignia of great houses or even museums was often stamped on the buttons of hall-porters or doormen. Apparently a Birmingham firm in the 19th century held no less than 10,000 different dies at one period for stamping these livery buttons.

Firemen, whether they belonged to voluntary brigades or to the Fire Insurance Companies in the early 19th century, wore rather military uniforms which were frequently decorated with brass buttons to match their brass helmets. Railway guards were still proudly wearing silver buttons in the 1860's. In the 1840's whereas a Superintendent also sported silver buttons, lesser fry only wore metal ones.

District messengers, with smart little pill-box hats worn at an angle and strapped under their chins, had metal buttons all down their blue serge tunics from the end of Queen Victoria's reign until as late as about twelve years ago. They looked like a page-boys of an earlier period; though these useful servants of large households, called 'Buttons', did not replace their top-hats with pill-box caps until about 1890. A page-boy's buttons were partly useful and partly ornamental. Sometimes he wore as many as three rows of cone-shaped buttons down his jacket. Mayhew with characteristic felicity of style described them in 1847 as being 'as close together as a rope of onions'.

The coster, or barrow-boy's pearly buttons began to decorate his waistcoat in the mid-19th century. He had always been a showy dresser, and sometimes his waistcoat buttons were of brass as well as the customary mother-of-pearl, which subsequently covered the whole of his clothes and those of his wife and family as well on festive days, harking back to the days of Henry VIII as we have seen.

In the 19th century the 1860's and 1870's were what has been called 'the great button era' as far as women were concerned. The cloth button with an iron shank was invented by 1825 and buttons made of wood or mother-or-pearl began to appear in the 1830's. Ornamental and useful buttons began to make their appearance on feminine clothes by the 1850's. They were made of metal and glass or covered with material and the new idea of a detachable button held by a pin was an innovation of this period. By 1860 oxydized silver buttons joined the variety and silk covered ones as well. A dress of 1861 shows the whole centre panel decorated by buttons starting at the neck the size of a pea and ending at the hem nearly as big as a saucer.

Next came square buttons made of pearl, tortoiseshell or ivory; by 1866 fashion decreed large buttons of oxydized silver and jet, whilst some had classical heads in relief and others the key pattern inlay. By now they were fit to be classified as jewellery and were made of fancy gimp, cameos, open-work iron, enamel and jet as well as those of pearl, ivory and tortoiseshell. And they were huge.

In 1886 fashion magazines mention smoked pearl buttons, and 'the kernel of the corozo nut' and rosary beads were being used for trimmings. A rather bizarre touch described in one magazine is 'a miniature pair of tongs in diamonds holding a ruby to represent a redhot coal'. This of course was a brooch and not a button and is only introduced by the way as it is so amusingly 'period'. Whilst we are on the subject, the fashion for earrings in the form of 'monkeys, saucepans, lizards, candelabra, cockroaches, bird-cages and tortoises' appears to have come to us from America.

Wooden buttons are not to be despised, and there are some delightful examples carved from walnut, bog oak and other woods, some set with gem-cut quartz, others carved like animal heads, some painted, some inlaid and even transfer printed. By the way, a sad habit nowadays, which spoils their value and attractiveness, is to make antique buttons into brooches or earrings.

The history of buttons, is a fascinating and rewarding study, but only in museums can the golden buttons of Ancient Egypt, Mycenae, Herculaneum and Troy be found. There were decorative buttons of amber, bronze, wood and bone in pre-Christian days and there was one German archaeologist who believed that Neolithic man wore stone buttons as long ago as 4000 B.C.

As a status symbol a 19th century American wore diamonds to button up his underclothes, presumably to impress his valet and his lady friends. Louis XIV, according to Saint Simon, could hardly stand upright for the weight of diamonds on his clothes, an inventory of his diamond buttons reaching astronomical figures. Other European kings and noblemen needless to say tried to follow his example.

There are many erudite books on the subject and sets of sporting buttons, the Victorian Aesop's fables, the Kate Greenaway children and animal, bird and reptile sets are all avidly collected. French buttons have such attractions as miniature paintings on ivory, satin or paper which are mounted under glass with a metal backing on a shank. Apparently these lovely decorative buttons are to be found in France without too much difficulty. In the Musée Carnavalet in Paris there is a splendid set of French Revolutionary patriotic buttons. As for America, the ones that were worn in honour of George Washington when he was inaugurated in 1789 are very much desired. These were made of copper or brass by hand and are engraved with his initials surrounded by 'Long Live the President' and similar heartening sentiments. Other

33

buttons commemorating Grant, Andrew, Jackson and even Eisenhower can be found.

Wedgwood did not fail to exploit the interest of Victorian ladies in ceramic buttons, jasper-ware cameos being his particular contribution to this tiny art form; and much later Fabergé did not disdain to enchant us with enamel buttons; and although they are very rare at least we can visit museums to enjoy looking at exquisite examples from Limoges and Battersea.

Another type of button which is much collected in America is the Navajo Indian 19th century silver one. The Indians used these as currency, pawning them if necessary, just as the Dutch explorers used to use their huge silver buttons as currency much earlier in history.

Glass buttons, made in the 1840's by the French glass factories which produced those exquisite paperweights, are rare prizes to find. Sometimes they have a lovely Clichy rose captured under a bubble of glass, or else a sulphide portrait or the same flower canes used for the beautiful paperweights.

The choice in this miniature field is very wide and already the National Button Society of the U.S.A. has been in existence for about 25 years fostering the preservation of this delightful minor art.

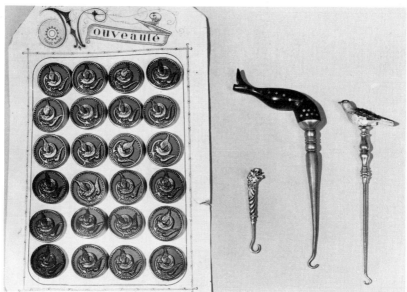

The French buttons are dated 1870. The leg button hook is the earliest of the three, the small silver tiger-head is marked 1903; the robin c. 1910.

Eight out of sixteen French 18th century buttons of
'Monuments of Paris'. They are printed on paper under
the glass faces, slightly retouched with gouache, in
copper frame.
(*from the collection of Monsieur Victor Houart*)

Set of six different 18th century French steel buttons,
c. 1795. Flat steel engraved by hand, applied bronze
figures in high relief. They are probably representing
songs or stories. One bears the words 'Au clair de la lune'.
(from the collection of Monsieur Victor Houart)

Set of four seasons on porcelain, transfer on hand-
painted gold background.
(from the collection of Monsieur Victor Houart)

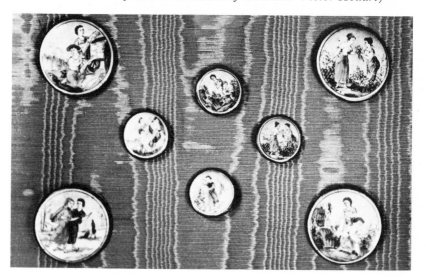

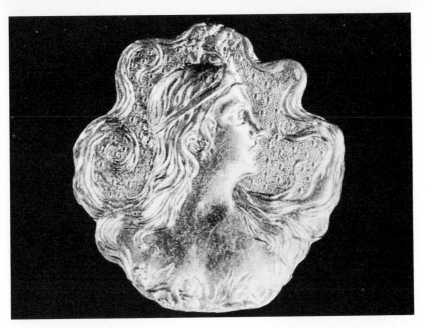

Beautiful metal Art Nouveau buttons. These buttons
of the 1900 period are becoming rare collector's pieces.
Monsieur Houart considers these are the last truly
collectable buttons.
(from the collection of Monsieur Victor Houart)

The elegant 18th century button is from a set of the
Italian Comedy. The miniature is hand-painted on
ivory under glass, with a trimming of cut steel.
(from the collection of Monsieur Victor Houart)

II
Shoe Buckles

They were first fashionable in 1659, and for the next 150 years nearly every man, woman and child wore them; but what seems difficult to come by is any information about the why, when or where they originated. There were silver buckles on Englishmen and women's shoes in the 15th and 16th centuries.

Pepys certainly liked to keep abreast of fashion and on January 22nd, 1659, he noted, 'This day I began to put buckles on my shoes' and there is also a reference to them in Evelyn's diary about this time. They were taking the place of the enormous roses which were previously so fashionable on gentlemen's shoes. At first buckles were small, 'not unlike a bean in shape and size' records a contemporary writer. By 1750 they had become enormous and by 1774 they were very showy indeed, decorated with jewels and especially diamonds, for those who could afford them, and paste for the rest.

There is a well-known story about a sixth form boy at Westminster School in the 1690's. The headmaster, a notable scholar called Mr. Busby, gave his boys an essay to write on the Latin phrase, *Fronti nulla fides*, or things aren't always what they seem. One boy did not sit down like the rest and begin to write. 'Why,' asked the Doctor, 'are you standing looking at your shoe-buckles instead of writing your essay?' 'I've done it,' replied the boy. 'These buckles to be silver you have rated; but *fronti nulla fides*, they are plated.'

The beginning of the 19th century brought the eclipse of the buckle on shoes, though a brief flowering came in Edwardian days, but never again was there a fashion in the true sense of the word, though buckles are still worn on shoes for ceremonial occasions. The Highlander regiments and Chieftains' dress include shoe-buckles and they are worn by the Lord Chancellor, the Lord Chief Justice and the Speaker, but these are only rather dull little steel patterns. The high Church dignitaries like Archbishops and bishops wear silver shoe buckles on State occasions and foreign ecclesiastics used to wear huge silver buckles on their shoes, and still may do so for all I know.

The variety of sizes and materials in which collectors may find buckles is quite large. They were made by the million in Birmingham and Wolverhampton and Walsall in the 18th century and exported to Italy, Spain, Germany, France, Holland and even to America. By 1790, however, the Prince of Wales was petitioned by the manufacturers of these towns to assist them by furthering the fashion in shoe buckles by using them himself instead of 'shoe-strings'. The Prince was as good as his word and introduced an outsize buckle one inch long and five inches wide. Perhaps the very grandeur of such a Brobdingnag of a shoe-buckle defeated its purpose, for nobody appears to have followed Prinny's lead. In any case he had only tried to resuscitate his father's fashion for these wide rectangular buckles across the instep that George III wore at his Coronation in 1761.

There are shoe-buckles made of steel, silver and gold, pinchbeck, enamel and silver-plate even tin and other metals, and those that were decorated with diamonds or paste, emeralds, topaz and other precious gems. Of course there have been buckles for other purposes like the band of a hat or to tether the belt or to fasten knee-breeches or an 18th century stock. The first quarter of the 19th century saw a vogue for ladies' belt buckles. However, here we have decided only to discuss those worn on shoes. One has to draw the line somewhere.

MINIATURE CLOTHES

Sales catalogues now always include an inventory of the clothes of the dolls they are selling, as this is an extremely important part of their attributes. If the clothes are good and above all contemporary to the doll this will help to get a good price for the seller.

A Bru or Jumeau fashion doll, for instance, with her bisque head and shoulders, her ears pierced and wearing earrings and with fixed blue paperweight eyes and a kid body, might be wearing a blue silk dress trimmed with white lace and matching hat, and perhaps carrying a parasol. If she has in addition a trunkful of elaborate clothes and bonnets, work-basket, jewellery, photograph album, shoes, underclothes and brush and comb, the doll would at least double its price. But most of the trunks to be found have been rifled of their contents long ago, and we are lucky if we find dolls provided with an extra dress or two nowadays. The trunks are little works of art, even if they are empty, with their domed lids to accommodate hats packed on the tray which would also be used for lighter things like stockings, gloves and handkerchiefs, the heavier boots and shoes being laid on the bottom of the trunk.

Dolls' house dolls do not usually have a trousseau of clothes, but one of my early 19th century dolls, dressed in an azure blue dress with the full upper sleeves of the late 1820's and a turban on her painted wooden head, also brought with her a straw-coloured dress with enormous sleeves and tucks on the wide hem and a charming green poke bonnet with a high crown and ribbons. The doll is about four inches high.

A pedlar doll, with her trayful of knicknacks, is the same period, circa 1830 or a year or so earlier. She wears exactly the same type of turban and a wide upper sleeved dress as the smaller doll and her skirt is of black velvet with a lace apron over it.

A much later acquisition was three little bisque-faced dolls with wigs and sleeping eyes, all about 6 inches high. They had belonged to an old lady, now nearly ninety years old, and they had a basketful of tiny clothes fitted with hooks and eyes. One dress was knitted in very fine cream wool by 'Aunt Clara' and it fits particularly well. There is a red-riding hood cloak and bonnet, a blue silk and lace party frock and several other minute garments, which now hang in a dolls' house wardrobe. Presumably they all date circa 1885–90.

On a larger scale there are the beautiful fashion doll clothes we have already mentioned, of which few survive off the dolls themselves, though they may well be in private hoards of dedicated collectors who, although they have not a doll who fits the clothes, nevertheless cannot, understandably, bring themselves to part with these miraculous small dresses, coats, hats, gloves, shoes and accessories.

The costume museum at Bath displays not only a magnificent collection of adult and children's clothes dating from the 18th century to the 1930's, but also shows a variety of dolls and their furniture and a particularly fine group of dolls clothes. The care and ingenuity lavished on these little garments shows how skilled and painstaking were children and of course governesses and mothers and aunts and cousins of the past. Well, they had a lot of time, those who were well-off at least.

The 18th century crèche clothes occasionally appear in the open market. These were used for dressing nativity scenes or perhaps shrines which were a particular feature of Italian life. The figures that were dressed in the clothes were generally of painted wood or their bodies might be made of wire wrapped round with rags to enable the setter of the religious scene to arrange them more easily into different attitudes. The clothes were not always made to take on or off, and these of course are of little interest to collectors, except insofar as materials and their dates are important. The Victoria and Albert Museum's textile department has materials in chronological order mounted in glass frames which is a great help to researchers in this field.

The fashionable doll of the early 18th century was provided with little garments which must have been given the same care as the contemporary samplers. They certainly helped small girls to embroider, to stitch with infinite patience and skill, to trim the

18th century clothes for crèche figures; made of velvet,
trimmed with gold embroidery, probably Neapolitan.

tiny caps and cuffs with pillow-lace; and it is interesting to read
even earlier that the cambric used for the huge ruffs of the courtiers
was so delicate that 'the greatest thread was not so big as the
smallest hair that is'.[1]

[1] *Anatomie of Abuses* by Philip Stubbs, 1595.

Some exquisite little pieces of needlework made by young women of the 18th century for their dolls include lace-trimmed mittens an inch long, and equally small kid ones with long gauntlets and stitched on the backs with silk, the inside of the hands lined with patterned linen. Quilted linen forms a little sleeveless bodice not as much as four inches long. There are caps and cuffs, shoes made of silk and kid, and that special glory for any doll, some really smart hats, which are also made of silk or even of a tiny basket-weave trimmed with ribbons, flowers and lace. These lovely clothes were fitted on to treasured wooden dolls and the colours of the brocades and silks, the elegant little pink woven silk stockings with floral clocks embroidered on them, and even tiny garters to keep up the stockings, and the embroidered shoes are almost too minute to believe that human eyes unaided by strong glasses could possibly work anything so fine. Take a look, for instance, at the inhabitants of the Uppark baby house and also at the curtains and the bed-hangings there.

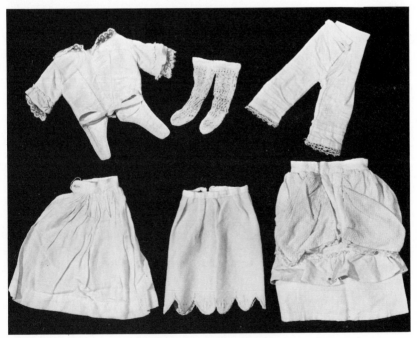

A cream-coloured fine wool dress for an adult doll, with underclothes. Second half of 19th century.

The males of the period are equally resplendent and wear velvet coats, impeccably cut and stitched, with knee breeches and tiny leather latchet shoes. One grand nobleman wears a suit of beige corded silk and the coat is fastened with miniature blue buttons.

As for the underclothes of the treasured dolls of the past, just as much care and ingenuity was lavished on these. The collector will be very unlikely to find these very early clothes and dolls, but the 19th century is quite a treasure house of beautiful needlework too. There are tiny samplers which grace dolls' house walls and these were obviously an apprenticeship before tackling first dolls' clothes and then something more ambitious on the adult scale.

Underclothes throughout the 19th century was very plain and simple both in design and material when compared with the elaborate care lavished on the dresses, coats, bonnets, hats and accessories. The hem of the petticoat might be embroidered because it was likely to be seen occasionally, and stockings were sometimes embroidered round the ankle which would show. There was an odd period in the 1880's which went on roughly until the 1930's when a pair of silk stockings might have cotton tops and soles to the feet. A magazine of the 1890's even went so far as to warn its readers, 'No nice-minded lady would think of wearing expensive underclothing.' From the late 1850's until nearly the end of the century a nice warm red petticoat was worn and up to the 1880's white was always worn 'next to the skin'. By the 1870's a tendency for coloured vests and 'drawers' cheered up the husbands no doubt, and corsets were tightly laced round the rather unnecessarily full chemises. It must have taken women a very long time to put on and fasten up all their layers of chemises, corsets, petticoats and drawers. These last were an addition to female clothes which caused quite a flutter, as they were after all the prerogative of the male sex. The theft of trousers for women's wear is so common now that the reaction of the general public at the turn of the 18th century is quite a surprise to us today. A French comment on their appearance as early as 1783 is sharp, 'Sauf les actrices les Parisiennes ne portent point de caleçon.' Yet, by 1850 they were almost a symbol of good breeding. A contemporary letter called them 'those comfortable garments

44

which we have borrowed from the other sex, and which all of us wear but none of us talk about'. They were not however adopted by the average woman until the 1880's. A lady-in-waiting to Queen Victoria described how the Duchess of Manchester tripped as she navigated a stile in her crinoline in 1859. The revelation of a pair of scarlet tartan knicker-bockers, 'the things Charlie shoots

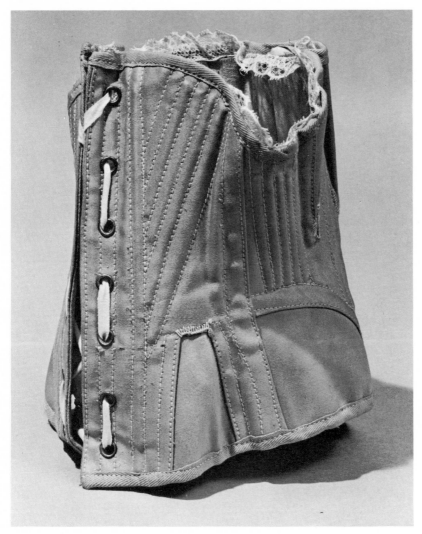

Doll's corset, *c.* 1850; it is about 8 inches high.

in', caused the Duc de Malakoff to say later, '*ma chère, c'était diabolique*'.

To return to our miniature underclothes, however, dolls are less *risqué* in their apparel. In the 1820's they wear a short sleeved chemise with a gusset under the arm, quite unshaped otherwise, and an unsleeved petticoat of cotton; muslin was for evenings and might have short puffed sleeves. The dolls may have drawers, as children used to wear them. A magazine of 1808 notes, 'It is now ... the fashion to dress children, both boys and girls, in pantaloons instead of petticoats.' These were worn under the frocks and were made of calico or in winter of flannel. By the 1820's and 1830's the long trousers remained a part of girls and boys dress beneath their frocks; then by the 1850's they became shorter and shorter and disappeared from sight by 1860. From being called generally trousers, now they were termed underclothes or drawers.

Dolls are sometimes found dressed in Highland dress as the fashion for these Scottish suits was started by the Royal children who were painted in it by Winterhalter in 1849. The vogue lasted for twenty years from that date, so collectors must look for other signs as well to date their dolls.

The knickerbocker suit also became popular through the Prince of Wales. During the 1860's, according to the *Englishwoman's Domestic Magazine 1861–2*, little boys of six and seven years old wore sailor's hats and a sailor's blouse with square collar and knickerbockers. This style too had a long life in various guises and although boy-dolls are rarer than girls they reflect this fashion in their miniature clothes.

In the 1840's little girls were sometimes forced to wear stays 'to train the figure' and the long attenuated figures of some dolls of this period, with their tiny waists bear witness to this painful and indeed dangerously unhealthy practice amongst the ultra-fashionable set. By the 1860's boned stays were being frowned on by more sensible mothers.

Girls of the 1860's were dressed like small versions of their mothers and this too is mirrored in dolls' clothes, for the elegantly dressed lady-dolls began to appear shortly after this. A doll dressed as Alice-in-Wonderland, a lovely Jumeau, wears clothes that are exactly the replica of Tenniel's drawings of Alice with

46

charming striped socks and boots with square toes.

Miniature shoes and gloves both have considerable appeal and the French Parisienne dolls have beautifully made kid gloves that bear inspection under a magnifying glass to see the excellence of their cut and finish, complete with tiny pearl buttons the size of lentil seeds. Boots too, with perhaps scalloped flaps that have minute button holes to fit equally minute buttons, and neatly shaped heels are irresistible in their tiny perfection. This particular style was circa 1875.

A little paper-backed book dated 1896, and entitled typically 'Dolly's Dressmaker', was published by Raphael Tuck and Sons. It gives careful instructions on the making of miniature clothes; the patterns are to fit a doll 9 inches high. An apron; 'mantle' or unshaped coat with leg-of-mutton sleeves and trimmed with velvet and fur; several hats, petticoat, blouse, skirt and frock with yoke are all catered for and no trouble spared. Sleeves and capes

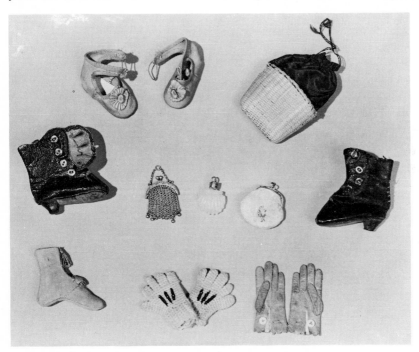

A selection of doll's shoes, boots, gloves and accessories;
19th century. The hand-stitched kid gloves were part of
a fashion doll's trousseau.

are lined, petticoats and dresses embroidered and pictures of the dresses with accessories like hairbands, hats, gloves, shoes and boots suggest further work for the budding dressmaker. Nowadays children, armed with pocket-money, buy ready-made clothes for their dolls. Hence the great demand for home-made clothes of the past.

Naturally the highest demand is for the little trousseaux made by *couturières* and occasionally there is a miraculous discovery of a trunk that has its original clothes and toilet necessaries, like brushes and combs, jewel-case, hand-mirror and so forth, intact.

Eighteenth century creche figure clothes in velvet
trimmed with gold embroidery. Probably Neapolitan.

Photo by Studio Wreford

MINIATURE CURIOSITIES

The most amusing quest is for those strange bygones which cause great speculation and interest and whose use is neither immediately apparent, nor always easy to solve. The unexpected oddity has the attraction of an archaeological find. The seeker expects to come across something unusual but is never quite sure what his digging will reveal. The small general antique shop or the market stall is our best hunting-ground, and the more obscure country or small town auction sales and private houses disposing of bric-à-brac.

Many delightfully bizarre finds have come my way, like the Victorian inkpot made from the stuffed head of an auk; and two other unusual birds, each handmade by some imaginative craftsman. One is a wooden snuff-box, shaped like a dove, carrying a painted leaf in its beak. The wings both flap open when a spring is pressed and another pressure on the bird's side causes the back wings to open and reveal the box inside for snuff. There is an inscription written through the penwork feathers in Russian, proclaiming peace in 1878. The second bird is also of wood, black and hard, probably ebony. It is inlaid with coloured circles of red and white ivory and its head is crowned with a rosette of red ivory. Its back is striped with inlaid ormolu and its ormolu wings slide up and down; the tiny legs are tucked under its breast and these can come down to enable the bird to stand up. In its body are two blades of steel. Is it a penknife? Is it a knife for eating with, or working with? I do not know. Everybody who has seen it makes suggestions, but nobody knows for certain. We all agree it is probably of Eastern European origin.

Quite a different piece of curiosa appeared in a local shop recently. This is a travelling candle-shield dated circa 1810. It fits neatly into a red morrocco case decorated with two anthemion or honeysuckle flowers, which was a Greek classical motif popular in England on silver, furniture and other articles from the second half of the 18th century and continuing during the Regency. Our case, about 6 inches long, opens to show three pieces neatly contained in three compartments. One expands into a silk fan forming a circle held by a brass tube. This fits into a second tube that in turn fits into the third piece, a movable clasp which grips the stem of the candle. The shade is then in a position to protect the reader's eyes from the full candle-light, throwing it on the book only. This ingenious device was patented in a slightly different non-travelling form in 1817 (patent No. 4132) and called 'Day's chimney ornament or fire screen'.[1]

A similar red morocco case like that of the candle-shield with two honeysuckle flowers, to match the top to the bottom, is shown in Eric Delieb's *Silver Boxes* (page 28). It contains a 'toothbrush, with removable brush-pad and plain tapering handle, double-ended tongue scraper and toothpowder box with double compartment . . .'.

Another aid for travellers was a pair of travelling brass candlesticks 4 inches in diameter contained in their saucers which screw together with the sockets inside. This handy invention, together with the candle-shield, would have been as easy to carry about as the delightful silver travelling sets, equally miniature, which were sometimes called campaign sets. These were often given to friends as gifts. For instance a silver-gilt set dated 1686, contained in a small shagreen case, resembling a doll-size hat-box, comprised a tumbler, a spoon, a knife and fork and a double spice-box. Round the rim of the little beaker were the words, 'A Bartlemew Fairing' and the name of the recipient and giver of this charming present. The Fair was of course Bartholomew Fair, a popular trading and shopping centre for all classes. Famous silversmiths rented booths there and well-known characters like Pepys would often go to pick up a gift for his wife, 'poor wretch', or a friend.

The travelling sets could of course be quite large and contain toilet flasks, toothbrushes, saucepans, coffee and tea sets and even a bell to summon the servant.

[1] See the Science Museum's booklet on *Lighting* by W. T. O'Dea.

Another bygone which, though in itself not miniature, contains small hidden objects in some instances. This is the outmoded walking stick. There are not many of these about, possibly because once discovered by a collector he does not easily part with such a delightful treasure.

Not only did our own Henry VIII possess a number of walking 'staves' but even right back in antiquity the boy-King Tutankhamen had made for himself a small collection of them. One of Henry VIII's sticks contained a surprising number of little objects. There was a dial and compass, a knife with a file and even a whetstone, as well as the more usual pouncet box. There are many sticks that conceal vinaigrettes and snuff-boxes, but not so often do we find the writing stick, with its useful ink-bottle, pen and pencils hidden inside it. There are drinking sticks too and these usually hold a long thin flask found halfway down and the knob unscrews to present a tiny glass goblet to drink from. These sticks were still being made in Germany at the end of the 19th century, but instead of being covered with a wood veneer, the later ones are only covered over the hollow cane with painted and varnished paper to simulate rosewood. Besides these already mentioned hidden uses, some walking-sticks contain horse-measures, dog-whistles, even spy-glasses and woodworking tools. Swords are quite common, and so are fishing-rods. For sturdy walkers there are compasses inside like the staves Henry VIII carried.

In 1807 a certain Edward Orme wrote a book called *An Essay on Transparent Prints*. The book was fully illustrated and it described in detail how to make what the Victorians called a 'transparency'. This remarkable kind of picture is decorative on your walls in its small way and also makes an interesting talking point which is useful with tongue-tied visitors. Essentially it was a coloured print which was mounted on a board and then pasted on top of another scene which showed through on being held up to the light. In the 1830's and 1840's there appeared two interesting series, one by Spooner called 'Spooner's Transformations', and the other by Morgan, called 'Improved Protean Scenery'. My own examples are very popular with new friends, and even those who know them well are pleased to look again. Napoleon, for instance, stands sadly on the seashore of St. Helena. What is he thinking about as the waves creep up the sand to his feet? We only have to hold the picture to the light and we see he is dreaming of the regiment of troops he is reviewing. Another picture has a beautiful pink rose like a *Redouté* print. Lift it up and look at it against a strong light and there in the rose sits the young Queen Victoria at her coronation. There are many sets of these curious bygones, but they are both rare and expensive now.

Once the search for curiosa has bitten a collector, he will become quite an addict and the ordinary run-of-the-mill antiques may stir his imagination no more. But this kind of collection is more for the antiquarian or historian, because oddities do not often found your fortune. They are too peculiar to be everybody's taste, and generally speaking it is having something that everybody else admires and wants which will bring in the hard cash.

This unusual oriental silver-mounted pumice-stone is said to have been used for shaving.

(*above*) A stirrup jug in the form of a hound and two miniature glass boots for stirrup cups.

(*left*) This unusual Minton joke-mug, mid-19th century, has a black-robed monk inside instead of the customary frog. He is hollow, with open mouth and there is a hole in the bottom of the mug.

53

Early 19th century workbox in the form of a house. The lid opens to reveal interior full of needlework accessories. There are two drawers.

An 18th century barber's powder-bellows with the glassmaker's example used for toilet-water.

DOLLS

I

Dolls in variety

Until comparatively recently children used to be dressed as miniature adults so the early dolls were also dressed in the grown-up clothes of the period. Lucky is the collector who can find a genuine 'Queen Anne' doll like the 18th century ones living in Uppark baby house, for instance. These hand-carved dolls are crudely made generally, with their faces and necks covered with a thin coat of gesso and then painted with bright cheeks, the dark brown glass pupil-less eyes inset, and sometimes dotted round the edge with spots to represent eyelashes and eyebrows. Their hands are like a five pronged fork and a piece of hair is nailed to the head. The clothes, made of the beautiful velvets, chintzes and printed calicos of the times, are seldom in good condition any more than the dolls themselves; but the smaller sized dolls that peopled the popular baby houses were more fortunate as they received special care since the houses were more for the pleasure of adults than playthings for the children.

There is something almost life like in these curious wooden dolls. They have the vitality of a primitive picture or an early Staffordshire 'image toy'. Mr. John Noble, Curator of the Toy Collection of the Museum of the City of New York, points out that they date as a type from as early as 1600, when their eyes were generally painted and their features more delicately carved, up to the wooden dolls with moulded plaster faces and painted eyes of the early 19th century.

A beautiful painted wooden doll circa 1740 was sold in 1969. She had brown glass eyes and a brown wig, of which a part was missing and so were some of her fingers as well as the top part of a leg. However, she was wearing her original clothes of a white chemise, a satin boned corset and an open dress and petticoat

55

Crèche figure in original clothes, probably late 18th
century from Italy.

made of red velvet with white stripes, probably taken from a man's coat of the period. The broken white stripes had figured black motifs and after 230 odd years the doll's extra green silk dress from an even earlier period and some extra pieces of the velvet from her gown were still with her. What a treasure she must be to own, with her contemporary record of clothes and styles. The Museum of Childhood in Edinburgh has a beautiful example of this type, wearing a little cap over her dark hair and a charming green silk dress with an apron. What character there is in this sulky little girl's face. She is dated circa 1750.

The 18th century wax dolls which inhabited dolls' houses had carefully modelled faces of considerable character. Wooden dolls' house dolls were generally dressed as servants, but the wax beauties' faces were so exquisitely modelled, just like religious ones for crèches or shrines, that they were given the rôle of mistress and master of the grand baby house in which they lived. Oddly enough their bodies were roughly made of stuffed cloth or even wire bound with bits and pieces of linen. The 18th century of course was carrying on the tradition of wax portraits, of which many beautiful examples can be seen in the Victoria and Albert Museum. Alas, these wax dolls, made in several sizes, were much more vulnerable to the ravages of time. Changes of temperature affect them badly, for instance, though not quite as badly as the waxed papier-mâché dolls of the 1840's onwards, which often have a fine network of cracks all over their faces. The glass eyes of these early waxed dolls were often moveable and attached to a wire that could be operated from their bodies. As they had real hair glued and pressed down into a slit in their heads these dolls are usually named 'splitheads'. My family doll called Augusta has dark corkscrew curls and a very rosy face. She wears a white satin dress with a low neckline and a sash, and mittens on her stuffed kid arms. Her legs and the body with its very wasplike waist, are also of kid. Sometimes the arms are coloured to represent gloves in these dolls, which are usually quite large, about 18 inches or more tall. They were occasionally put in glazed boxes with frames for display, and dressed as brides or with trailing sprays of flowers around them, and even with birds or butterflies in the case too. Of course this treatment ensured that they were far better preserved. There is, however, something rather sinister about

The baby cries and kicks his legs as the carriage moves.
The doll is wax over papier-mâché, *c.* 1850–60.

Wax-over-composition dolls in box, with flowers, fruit
and miniature sheep; 2nd half of the 19th century.
(Courtesy of Rupert Gentle)

'boxed dolls'. They have the power, like Madame Tussaud's waxworks, of giving some of us a chilled spine. They look horribly like miniature adults that have been provided with a shrunken-head treatment all over. This of course is sacrilege; but Vivien Greene, whose book on English dolls' houses is now a collectors' piece, shares my view.

'Pumpkin-heads' are the later version of this type of doll. About 1860, or perhaps a little earlier, the papier-mâché dolls' heads were waxed right over a modelled hairstyle giving them the shape which somebody has christened 'pumpkin'. Occasionally they wear hats as well, which are also coated over with wax. They have wooden arms and legs and often a squeaker concealed in the stuffed-cloth body, and they come in several sizes. Since nobody has yet bothered to fake them they are quite a good line to collect, even if their simple homely appearance does not appeal to everyone.

The Motschmann babies made in Sonneberg were also imported from Japan. They have jointed composition heads and arms and legs on a stuffed twill body and my example has black glass eyes and a paper sewn on its contemporary clothes saying in spidery faded ink, 'I was bought in London in 1851', presumably at the Great Exhibition.

The enormous variety of materials in which dolls have been made is quite a headache for collectors once they reach the 1840's. This was the date when the waxed doll we have just discussed appeared on the scene and so did the painted papier-mâché doll. The china heads mostly made their début towards the end of the 1840's. These last are often very beautiful and the rare early ones may be marked by such famous factories as Meissen and Nymphen-burg and other continental firms. They vary from dolls' house size to quite large ones. Glazed china heads made specially for the doll factories soon appeared and though their hair styles can approximately date them, it is as well to remember that the same mould might be used for several years. In fact this glossy china head was made right up until the First World War.

The elegant bisque, or unglazed china dolls[1] appeared towards the end of the 1850's. They came from Germany and Paris chiefly; neither England nor America produced them until the 20th century. The German and French ones were made in a great

[1] Sometimes called Parian or Parian-bisque.

many sizes and the ones with moulded hair and glass eyes, sometimes wearing lustre boots, are charming. Their varied hair styles are of special interest to collectors.

There is one group much neglected and therefore cheap at present. This is the so-called 'bisque baby' or bathing doll from one to eight inches high made between about 1870 to 1890. Others, much less attractive and often coarsely made were called Frozen Charlottes and these solid china dolls were made in the same sizes as the 'bisque babies' from about 1850 till 1914.

The aristocrats of the bisque class, which date from 1860, are the Parian-bisque beauties with French kid bodies that are jointed or gussetted at the shoulders and elbows and at the legs, thighs and knees. They have natural hair wigs and are beautifully dressed; their clothes are of the latest fashion down to the last detail, even originally including a trunk with a complete wardrobe inside. These are often known as 'Parisiennes' and they are associated with such famous 'Maisons' as Peronne, Huret[1] and, probably best

A collection of 19th century dolls. Four are of poured wax; two Parisiennes by F. G.; two bisque-headed dolls in Scandinavian costumes; two wax-over-composition dolls with moulded hair; a Motschmann-type baby 'bought in London in 1851'; mid-19th century rag dolls with paper hands in national dress; enamelled face wooden dolls c. 1830–40 and others. All are in original clothes.

[1]She applied for a patent for swivel-necks in 1861, beating Jumeau.

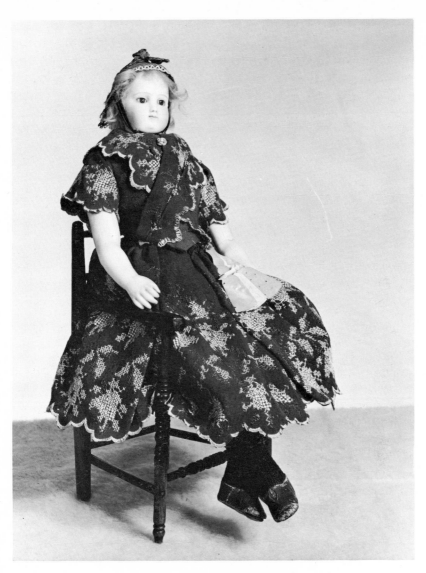

A Jumeau doll with bisque head and arms, and original
clothes and under clothes.

known of all Jumeau (1842–99). The Jumeau firm, after winning a bronze medal at the 1851 Great Exhibition for their dolls' wardrobes and medals in Paris in 1855 and London again in 1862 and many others later, finally joined a group called S.F.B.J. (*Société Française de Fabrication de Bébés et Jouets*) in 1899. Some of the Jumeau

Late 18th century automatic mandolin-player.
(*Courtesy of the Musée des Arts et Métiers, Paris*)

moulds which had been created by Emile Jumeau, were no doubt part of the deal. Collectors can now consult an excellent Encyclopaedia of Dolls compiled by D. S., E. A., and E. J. Coleman.

One exasperating difficulty for doll-collectors is the faker or 'restorer' at work. The restorer is fair enough, except that most collectors prefer to do or to supervise their own restoration; but faking is another matter. The Parisiennes are special targets for this practise and modern firms are producing very beautiful dolls that could well be collected in their own right if they were not made in order to deceive the unwary into buying them at antique values. Their dresses are made rather badly out of old materials, but two pointers to their age are the wigs and the curious auburn eyebrows. Remove the wig if in doubt and inside it will probably be stuffed with modern French or Italian newspaper. The kid body is suspiciously clean.

English dolls were made chiefly in London, Wolverhampton and Birmingham. We are best known for our wax dolls, but this is due to the fact that Italian families of doll-makers lived in England and we get reflected glory from such expert modellers as the Montanaris, Pierottis and Bazzonis.

II

Dolls' House Families

The splendid baby houses of the 17th and 18th centuries housed doll families made chiefly of wax and of wood. The Germans, with characteristic thoroughness, made the first of these exquisite mansions, it is now believed, and the Dutch were not long behind them. Every domestic detail was carried out in miniature with the same exactness which, three hundred years later, was lavished on the dolls' house given to Queen Mary. The city of Nuremberg cherishes some fine examples of this diminutive art and the beautiful Dutch cabinets are famous world-wide. To see the replicas of everyday life, peopled by tiny inhabitants in contemporary dress is quite a magical experience reminding us of Henry Janes's story called A Sense of the Past. His hero, standing in Berkeley Square in the late 19th century suddenly finds himself in the shoes of his ancestor and in the days of Sir Joshua Reynolds. The same clock ticks on the mantelpiece but the noises outside are the sounds of the 18th century. Artistic licence of course excluded the 18th century smells and squalor, thank goodness.

The dolls of this imaginary world of 18th century adults were beautifully made and clothed with great exactitude. They are about four or five inches high and all play their part in bringing the little rooms to life. In a Dutch house dated 1670 there is a cosy domestic scene of the husband and wife taking wine and tea respectively, the portraits of the ancestors are hanging on the wall and a half-open cupboard reveals the table linen. The husband keeps on his hat indoors which was customary. The wife is dressed in a beautiful stiff-silk robe over an embroidered petticoat. Both dolls are made of wax.

As far as present day collectors are concerned these dolls are only to be seen in museums and a few stately homes. The earliest we are likely to find at all easily are the delightful little wooden personages that Queen Victoria, helped by her governess Baroness Lehzen, so enjoyed dressing and giving names to, just in the same way that Anne Sharp, Queen Anne's god-daughter, gave names to the wax and wooden dolls in her baby house of 1700 that the Queen had given her.

The dolls are a complete family in this nine room town house and the owner 'My Lord Rochett' and his wife 'Lady Rochett' are served by 'Mrs. Hannah, ye House-keeper' and 'Roger ye Butler'. Their son and heir 'William Rochett' has a parrot in its cage and that popular animal of the period a monkey, in shovel-shaped hat, as playmates. The wax baby is too young to be much use to him, lying in a walnut cradle ornamented with ivory fret-work. The other child, a wax girl-doll, and her maid are both dressed in elaborate clothes with lace ruffles. A dolls' dolls' house of cardboard is a specially endearing touch. The servant dolls are wood, the owners are made out of wax, by the way.

Wooden dolls have a long ancestry dating back to the 15th century in Germany, the home of wooden toys. In their peg-wooden form they were made from the late 18th century in sizes ranging from half an inch to over two feet, until the early 20th century. They came from Grödner Tal in Austria, and they are beautifully jointed, even the ones half an inch high. They are not to be compared with the roughly made modern Dutch doll, which often has no joints at its elbows or knees, and a face stereo-typed to a couple of dots for eyes and, beneath a slight protuberance

A collection of nineteenth-century dolls, four of
poured wax; two Parisiennes fashion dolls of bisque by
F.G.; bisque headed dolls in Scandinavian costume;
wax-over-composition dolls with moulded hair; a
Motschmann-type body bought in 1851 in London;
rag-dolls mid-nineteenth century with paper hands;
wooden dolls c 1830-40 with enamelled faces, all in
contemporary clothes.

Photo Studio Wreford

for a nose, another dot in red for a mouth. The early 19th century Dutch dolls have painted faces and shoulders, which are varnished to look almost like enamel and their expressions are varied and delightful. They wear red or orange slippers and their hands are shaped like fish tails. Sometimes they are given a painted black topknot with a hair comb and they wear earrings. The earliest ones have black hair with grey wisps painted round the forehead.

A search for these dolls has the added spice of rarity. A windfall tumbled into a collector's hands a year or so ago when a telephone caller offered a boxful of old wooden dolls, all dressed, and varying in size from half an inch to about six inches high. What a splendid family for a Regency dolls' house. It turned out that there were no less than twenty of these unusual miniatures, dressed in periods from about 1820 to 1840, and some of them wearing minute bonnets and straw hats. They now inhabit a very small two-room cottage of a rather later date, until the early one turns up at a reasonable price.

Dolls' house dolls that are quite easily found are the glazed china-headed dolls, made in Germany, with stuffed bodies and rather roughly made arms and legs attached. The heads have black hair in various styles and they make excellent inhabitants for 19th century dolls' houses. Commercially made dolls, of small size date from circa 1875 onwards, and were advertised in family groups like, 'Fine dressed little dolls for doll rooms'.[1] They were about five to seven inches high and the best were of bisque, with moulded hair and painted shoes and dressed in period clothes. Some came from Germany and some from France, these last being more richly turned out. Some had glass sleeping eyes, others had real hair wigs and jointed arms and legs at the body, so they can sit conveniently on dolls' house chairs. Very small dolls in crochet clothes came from Germany and were bazaar goods found until 1914 in the shops and presumably old stock was still being sold during the First World War. Edwardian gentlemen complete with flowing moustaches are to be found and also boy-dolls, but they are rarer than the female sex.

[1] *Encyclopaedia of Dolls.*

E

III

Dolls in Pictures

An interesting approach for collectors is to go to our museums, galleries and stately homes and look for pictures with children holding or playing with dolls. This is one of the best ways of getting contemporary evidence and many museums nowadays also show dolls and their clothes. François Boucher (1703–70) painted an enchanting picture in 1739 which is in the Louvre. It shows a little girl clutching a horse on wheels in one hand and a lovely wooden doll in adult clothes, a wide skirt, an apron and be-ribboned cap and a bow tied under her chin. Much earlier Lucas Cranach (1472–1553) painted a picture called Charity, which is in our National Gallery. This shows another little girl cradling a doll in her arms. She herself being completely bare.

Some early fashion dolls of the 14th century were sent to little Princess Isabella of France when she was seven years old and married Richard II of England. These dolls were in several sizes, and the largest were as big as the little princess herself. Later, in 1600, Henry IV of France sent some 'model dolls', as he described them, to his future bride, Marie de Medicis. They were probably intended to show her what fashions French ladies were wearing, so that she should arrive in suitably up-to-date gowns and not in old-fashioned attire like the unfortunate Portuguese princess bride of Charles II of England, who arrived, much to all the courtiers' scorn, in a de-moded farthingale.

There is a famous portrait of Lady Arabella Stuart, painted when she was not yet two years old, wearing a white satin dress trimmed with pearls and holding her doll, probably a discarded fashion doll, which is dressed magnificently in crimson brocade with a green kirtle, and large ruff round the neck. The artist is unknown.

Another well-known picture including a doll is also in the National Gallery. It was painted by W. Hoare and shows Christopher Anstey sitting at a table writing a letter with a quill pen whilst his excited little daughter shows him her doll, also doubtless a discarded fashion doll, which is wearing an enormously high and elegant coiffure capped with feathers in 18th century style.

Nearer our times is a Victorian picture by W. Mulready called

The Toy Shop. This shows a poor little girl in rags who has set down her heavy basket and stares wonderingly at the window of a shop carrying a label 'Wax and Rag Dolls'. The doll dressed like a queen, with long fair hair and a crown, is what has caught the child's imagination.

The painter Renoir (1841–1919) drew a charming family group in which a little girl, very grandly dressed, is holding an equally elegant doll in the height of fashion. She looks as though she is made of wax and she has delightful striped stockings like Alice in Wonderland, dating her to the late 1860's. Of course the doll could be a lot earlier than the picture, and her clothes.

In the 17th century dolls were presented as luxurious and fashionable playthings to royal ladies. This habit continued until our own times when George VI and Queen Elizabeth were given dolls with handsome trousseaux for their daughters in 1938 when they visited Paris. These dolls were representations of the two princesses.

One English family followed an Eastern custom and dressed dolls in fashionable clothes from 1754 up to 1912, keeping them as family heirlooms and dating them carefully, finally giving them as a wonderful record of dress to the Victoria and Albert Museum.

FANS

I

French Fans

That inveterate collector of beautiful porcelain, pottery and *objets de vertu*, Lady Charlotte Schreiber, made a collection of foreign fans. Probably the height of their excellence was reached in France in the 18th century, one of their chief attractions being the delicacy of the painting and decoration. They must have originally been a form of fly-swat, to judge by their name *esmouchoir*, and of course the fans of antiquity were enormous, mounted on poles for the servants to fan their masters' heads. Henry II of France had the small *éventail* cut out like a lace pattern from vellum. A beautiful allegorical fan of the early days of the 18th century was painted on swan skin in rich and glowing colours. The mother-of-pearl sticks were enriched with gold, very finely worked. Tortoiseshell and ivory were also used for the sticks and highly decorated. In Louis XVI's reign the fashion was to ornament the silk fans with sequins. In the first half of the reign sticks were pieced together; later on they were separate. Most fans are not signed, so the pen-and-ink drawings on parchment that so vividly recall the life of the times, are unchronicled. Nevertheless, we are assured that such artists as Watteau, Fragonard, Boucher, Nattier and Greuze all painted fans and of course these can be attributed fairly certainly to the artists by the style, even though they are not signed. They were no doubt also copied by lesser artists. In fact the art of fan making became an industry in France and as early as 1678 there existed a Guild of Fan-makers. Queen Anne granted a charter in England to The Worshipful Company of Fan Makers in 1709.

The lavishness of workmanship expended on the sticks is a study in itself. They were made to overlap each other so that on being opened they presented a charming design, the ivory and

A French fan, 1860–70, with guards and sticks of carved ivory by Brisevi; the sticks also painted with groups of figures in the costumes of the period of Henri III. The mount is of lace. Made by Alexandre, this fan is an example of copying old styles in the 19th century.
(*Courtesy of the Victoria and Albert Museum. Crown Copyright*)

mother-of-pearl being carved and elaborately chased and inlaid with gold, silver and precious stones. The leaves of the fan were of leather, skin, or sometimes taffeta or parchment and all was covered with elaborate painting in brilliant colour. One described as having belonged to Queen Eleanor in 1590 was inlaid with quite a ransom of precious stones. But this of course was a rarity.

To come back to the 18th century, the fan commemorated many historical and social events, like the marriage of Louis XV and Marie Leczinska and of the Dauphin and Marie-Antoinette. In England such artists as Angelica Kauffmann, Hogarth and Bartolozzi engraved fans with classical or mythological subjects. In France Madame de Pompadour favoured ivory blades encrusted with gold ribbons and bows and studded with pearls and diamonds.

By the time Louis XVI came to the throne silk, lace and painted medallions of figures or fruit and flowers appeared and the passion for rustic life as played out by Marie Antoinette and her ladies, meant that pastoral scenes and homely life festooned with ribbons was the style of the day.

69

Next, and here was the beginning of the end, came the satirist and political cartoonist to decorate the 'popular' fan, which was bought by every women at a price she could afford. Lampoons accompanied the caricatures, which were generally ill-natured and coarse, with disrespect openly shown towards the Royal Family and the Court. This type of fan heralded the death-knell of the monarchy in France. It became a weapon in the hands of the populace to castigate the Queen and the King. The sticks now were made of cedarwood strung together with ribbons. Even Charlotte Corday was traditionally supposed to have carried a fan in one hand and the dagger she plunged into Marat in the other. The Revolutionary fan was printed with Phrygian caps and Republican symbols and the cry of Liberty and Equality. Many French refugees to England came with a few trinkets and what they could salvage of their possessions. That is probably why so many beautiful French fans have appeared in collections over here. Certainly the fan never reached its graceful, elegant artificial-

This beautiful Italian fan was made *c.* 1700. Mount of a painting of Venus and Adonis.
(*Courtesy of the Victoria and Albert Museum. Crown Copyright*)

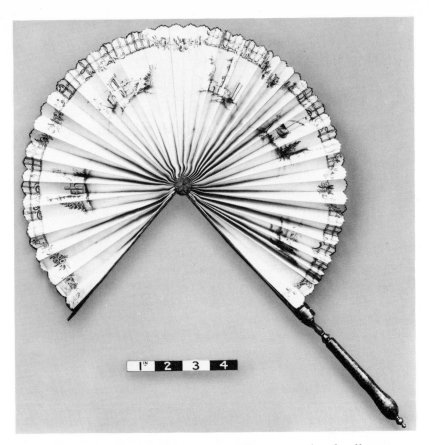

Here is an Italian fan, *c.* 1750. The mount is of vellum,
circular, with painted scenes of ruins, and a floral border.
Stick of steel inlaid with silver and gold.
(*Courtesy of the Victoria and Albert Museum   Crown Copyright*)

ity and luxury again. After the Revolution the fan lost its originality
to become a mere copy of past frivolous beauty and today, in spite
of our interest in antiques, the fan has rather unaccountably been
cold-shouldered by all except the discriminating few who prize
their treasures and care for them with the love of the true
connoisseur.

71

II

The Fan in England

Queen Elizabeth's portraits sometimes show her carrying a round fan made of feathers. The remarkable quota of 27 fans is listed in an inventory of her clothes in 1606. Probably they were easily worn out on account of the fact that they were used as a sort of semaphore to relay messages to lovers and rivals, thus playing an important part in the many Court intrigues. In fact the language of the fan became so intricate and subtle that a contemporary suggested that ladies of fashion should go through a course of 'fan drill' to keep them up to date in the complicated movements.

In the 18th century the elegant little fan called the 'minuet' came to England and these were flourished and waved about to the steps of the dance, adding greatly to the general effect of gracefulness and charm. They were usually ornamented with sequins of gold, silver or steel, and often encrusted with pearls and other precious stones. Carved mother-of-pearl sticks with lace, silk of vellum between them were particularly attractive. Others might have bone or ivory sticks pierced or carved with intricate designs.

When an Englishman called Joseph Child introduced a new carriage into Paris in 1755, it was called the cabriolet and soon became quite the fashion. In the same year Horace Walpole wrote, 'everything is to be *en cabriolet*. The men paint them on their waistcoats and have them embroidered for clocks on their stockings, and the women, who have gone all winter without anything on their heads, are now muffled up in great caps with round sides, in the form of, and scarce less than, the wheels of chaises.'

Naturally more femine counterparts had to be found and the cabriole fan was invented. It had a wide band at the top ornamented profusely and then a space which left the sticks uncovered; a second band of ornament filled in the rest of the fan, which was very large and usually mounted on skin, with perhaps gold, mother-of-pearl or jewelled encrustations. Often a looking-glass was inset into the fan's sticks so that the owner could observe what was going on without herself being observed. Fans were used as early as 1730 for 'quizzing' and the peepholes then were often covered with transparent material.

Small and unimportant fans were carried in the early 19th century, and in the 1840's handsome large fans were imported into England from China and France and Japan with scenes *à la Watteau* and carved ivory or mother-of-pearl sticks. There was a Fan Exhibition held at South Kensington in 1870, but of the seven or eight representative firms in London that showed their fans, only one of these was English. All the rest were French. It is not difficult to distinguish the 18th century fan from the 19th century pastiche. Comparison between two known examples are sufficient test.

The 1860's saw a revival in fans with steel sequins cut out in star shapes or flowers and silk painted with flowers, birds or figures. The magazines of the period advocate their use, urging fashionable women that their *toilette* would be incomplete without one.

Feather fans date to the 1870's and some later ones of the 1890's have the rather painful addition of a stuffed bird on their leaves, just as hats had at this period. Ostrich feather fans were popular from the late 1880's until the end of the century, and even into Edwardian days. 'Leaders of fashion,' remarks a women's magazine of 1887, 'prefer about sixteen magnificent ostrich feathers mounted on tortoiseshell.' The New York jewellers Tiffany and Co. made feather fans mounted on mother-of-pearl sticks. Sometimes fans with gaily coloured red and green feathers can be found, but their sticks are usually disappointingly of wood.

Lace fans can be dated by the type of lace used, Chantilly's bobbin lace in black silk being a favourite in the 1860's; and in the 1880's and 1890's there was Honiton lace, still made with bobbins but with no ground of net and the appliqué Honiton lace on machine-made net as well as the *point de gaze* or needlepoint lace. Nottingham lace was also used.

Some of the fans of the 1880's were enormous, about 16 inches long and these continued into the 1890's, followed by the so-called 'Empire fans', pale imitations of another epoch, itself in the decline.

In the 1880's there was a vogue for the Japanese and fans were often hung up on walls as decoration. A good many of these were made in England, though some were genuinely oriental. Throughout the Victorian period Chinese *brisé* fans made of ivory or wood

73

with intricately pierced patterns, were imported in various shapes and sizes.

Apart from the First World War and the advent of suffragettes probably electric lighting killed the fan, as gas and candlelight give more heat and the new century ushered in the draughts and fresh air so much deplored by our Continental friends.

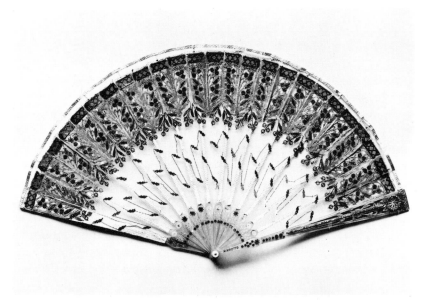

An English fan, *c.* 1800. The mount is of gauze with applied pierced steel decoration; sticks and guards of stained horn inlaid with steel.
(*Courtesy of the Victoria and Albert Museum   Crown Copyright*)

MINIATURE FURNITURE

Generally oak was the wood used for making furniture in England from very early times until early Georgian days. Elm and beech were used too and by the end of the sixteenth century walnut was sometimes employed. Looking at illuminated manuscripts it is evident that furniture was then painted and gilded; but little of this decoration has survived and small wonder, after so many years and the fluctuations of fashion.

Miniature pieces of such antiquity are rare outside museums, so it is to such London treasure-houses as the Bethnal Green Museum that we must go to see and even handle these small masterpieces. An oak gate-leg table less than 6 inches high is so well proportioned that a photograph gives the impression of a full-sized piece. That is the criterion of true excellence of workmanship. Another splendid example is an equally small writing table made of walnut and dated about 1690. It is so meticulously made, this craftsman's miracle of $5\frac{1}{2}$ inches high, that it has veneering on the main structure and tiny brass drop handles. The delicacy of touch and the keen eyesight of whoever made this little writing-table must have been remarkable. Another gem is a miniscule dumb-waiter made of mahogany. But this is larger and stands about 12 inches high. It was made in the early days of George III's reign.

In the eighteenth century there was still a craze for collecting small objects to display in cabinets. This passion had been in full swing from the last decade of the seventeenth century and continued for over a hundred years. The Dutch 'cabinets' are famous and a visit to Amsterdam and the Rijksmuseum would be enough to inspire any collector to search for miniatures. Those perfect replicas of the full sized furniture, porcelain, glass, silver and pewter, brass and copper objects are irresistible to most of us, even those impervious to the charms of 'baby houses', as dolls' houses used to be called. Everything needed in a full sized mansion was made to fit into these lilliputian dwellings and they have been cherished and preserved in many cases so that we can see and admire them in museums all over the world. Some of the furniture was designed by famous cabinet-makers like Chippendale. There were 'toy' makers of this miniscule work in the early eighteenth century and the Dutch obviously exported their little masterpieces as a trade card of the period advertises them amongst other trinkets. This same turner also informed his customers that he mended 'toys and trinkets', so these tiny treasures were certainly valued by their owners enough to have them repaired when necessary. Children, of course, would not have been able to play with such expensive trifles, except under supervision. The baby-houses of the seventeenth and eighteenth century were meant to amuse their elders. Towards the very end of the eighteenth century baby-houses were on their way to the nursery and their best use as children's playthings. The furniture was not, after this, made entirely by craftsmen but by the estate carpenter or by gifted amateurs and professional toy shops, finally becoming commercialized by about 1840.

In Regency days a delightful range of dolls' house furniture appeared which Mrs. Graham Greene, Curator of the first Dolls-House Museum in England, has immortally named 'dolls-house Duncan Phyfe',[1] after the American designer who built up a successful trade in New York about 1790. His designs were based on the Sheraton-Directoire style and he worked almost entirely in mahogany at first. Then, from 1830 onwards, he used rosewood which is simulated in dolls-house furniture of the time. He was fond of the lyre motif, which also appears in the tiny replicas. Collectors usually date this dolls-house furniture to about 1835–40. One of the best pieces is the miniature work-table.

Several different sizes of furniture were made, as can be seen at the Bethnal Green and London Museums. The height of a 'Duncan Phyfe' sabre-legged chair is about $2\frac{1}{4}$ inches high; the work-table, with the mirror-lined lid closed to make a table,

[1]*Duncan Phyfe:* born in Scotland 1768, went to New York in his teens, retired from business 1847, died 1854.

stands 3 inches high. A set of this furniture is in the National Museum of Wales, Welsh Folk Museum also. The next size is about two inches larger, and some of it has marble tops to tables, washstands and sideboards. Now a lot of commercially made furniture was coming from Germany, and very well made it was. Only by the end of the nineteenth century is mass-production bringing depressing standards of workmanship. It is worth mentioning that many little pieces of furniture were not necessarily intended for dolls-houses, though used for this purpose. We may find such objects as Tunbridge-ware pincushions masquerading as tiny chairs, étuis in the shape of a sideboard, watchcases made to look like long-case clocks and so forth. Needlework boxes must often have been rifled for furnishing the dolls-houses.

Oddities from the home-made mid-19th century homes are represented in my smallest house by a chair made of clove-sticks giving an excellent imitation of Queen Victoria's staghorn furniture at Osborne House. A leather thimble-case shaped like a trunk fits in excellently too, as well as an inch high three-legged souvenir table made of jet, the surface engraved with a picture of Whitby Abbey.

Mrs. Janes Toller has coined the expression second-size miniatures, in her excellent book *Antique Miniature Furniture in Great Britain and America*, for those very well-made cabinet-makers' samples or show-pieces, which are usually rather misleadingly called apprentice-pieces. They would either have stood in the shop windows to advertise what was to be sold, just as shoemakers might put brass shoes in their windows; or else they were taken by the cabinet-maker as travellers' samples when he set off on his rounds to his various patrons in order to discuss orders for furnishings. Some of this furniture was probably commissioned for dolls-houses or dolls and a number of very handsome and interesting sofas, chairs, bureaux, beds, tables and other pieces are to be found in sizes from say 12 inches to 17 or 18 inches high. The desirable 17th and 18th century ones in the Bethnal Green Museum are rarely seen for sale, however.

Next in size comes the attractive children's furniture and here, as in smaller sizes, the chair in a great variety of styles is the easiest to find. There are charming little bureaux and desks, cradles, even bookcases of the eighteenth century and high-chairs as well. These too are mostly museum pieces, though 19th century chairs are quite often seen in antique shops, and so are cots, from the lovely swinging ones, suspended from posts to the country-made hooded cots mounted on rockers.

Our present Queen's grandmother, Queen Mary was a great collector and miniatures of all kinds had a special appeal for her. Besides her own dolls-house which she had as a child and which is now in the London Museum, she was presented with the famous one now at Windsor Castle and too well-known to need describing here. Some tiny rooms of hers she gave to the Bethnal Green Museum and these were equipped with furniture made of ivory, certainly originating in the East and showing that filigree delicacy of workmanship we expect in this kind of miniature. There are tables, chairs, bookcases and many other elegant little pieces.

18th century miniature furniture with maker's mark 'Bebbe' on each piece. The chest is 7 inches high.

(*above*) These two sample chairs are illustrated in several price-books, *c.* 1860–70. Costing four shillings a chair for the 'double C balloon back' and eight shillings for the steamer-chair, or 'cane-back and seat folder', they both appear in a furniture catalogue dated 1872.
(*Courtesy of the Art Gallery and Museum, High Wycombe*)

(*left*) Doll's chair of the Second Empire period, with velvet seat.
(*Courtesy of the Musée d'Histoire de l' Education, Paris*)

A French 18th century toilet-table for dolls, complete
with brush, powder boxes and box for jewellery,
gloves, bottles, etc.
(*Courtesy of the Musée des Arts Décoratifs, Paris*)

MINIATURE GLASS

I

Friggers

Spun glass was made as long ago as two thousand years in Rome and Egypt, and subsequently by the Arabs and Syrians, the Venetians and the Germans. Beautiful little toys were created by travelling glassblowers for the amusement of people visiting country fairs, so demonstrating their virtuosity. They would carry a bundle of coloured glass canes and a little portable furnace which was heated by a tallow flame. Their exquisite little *tours de force* were of unbelievable delicacy; birds of paradise with long, graceful spun glass tails, spaniel dogs with glass curls on their ears and tails and perhaps a blue ribbon round their necks and sometimes cosily seated in a spun glass basket, and many other enchanting fantasies. A little girl called Emily Shore wrote in her journal in 1831 about the craftsman she saw at work in Bedfordshire. 'He made glass baskets, candlesticks, birds and horses,' she noted. 'He sat at a table and before him was a little furnace which contained a flame of intense heat, though it was only kept by a tallow . . . We bought a few minor things and there was an elegant and beautiful ship.'

These little ships were very popular, some small and some about 10 or 12 inches long, made out of drawn out twists of spun glass and sometimes with minute sailors scrambling up the rigging, made of opaque glass. Similarly birds at a fountain with opaque red flowers and green leaves, the birds decorated with crimson crests, are another example of the glassblowers' skill. There is an early 19th century ship in the Victoria and Albert Museum. A small bust made of glass with spun glass hair can be seen at the British Museum.

Though it does not appear to be known exactly when these 'friggers' were first made in England, it is least possible that the

81

French glassblowers employed at Nailsea, who introduced the Venetian *latticino*, may have had something to do with it. Already at Nevers in France there were beautiful table decorations being made from blown and spun glass in many colours (see illustration) during the 18th century, and examples of these can be seen in the *Musée des Arts Décoratifs* in Paris, as well as crèche figures and scenes in the same delicate medium. It is often said that these glass ornaments look as though they had been made from spun sugar, and certainly there was an affinity between the confectioners' art and that of the glassblower when he was showing off his skill by making 'friggers'.

Glass marbles are used now in the production of glass fibre and except that a high-speed machine is employed today, the actual hand principle was used by the Venetians in the 16th century. Originally these Italian craftsmen were making glass beads as well as marbles from rods of coloured enamel twists. The marbles used in the game of solitaire are often, sadly, replaced with dull looking mass-produced modern ones.

The Great Exhibition of 1851 exhibited a tie made from fine glass threads of opaque blue and white glass. At this period the animals, flowers, glass ships and birds on their fountains, surrounded

19th century miniature glass made from oddments left over at the end of the day's work and called by the glass-blowers 'friggers'.

A dinner-table centrepiece made at Nevers in their famous spun-glass in the middle of the 18th century.
(Courtesy of the Musée des Arts Décoratifs, Paris)

by a frothy sea of glass wool, were extremely popular. The spun glass birds, with their drooping pink, white and blue tails, were much admired as mantelpiece ornaments. What is most remarkable is that so many of these delicate, fragile little friggers still exist today.

II
Some other small glass pieces

The line drawn between the friggers which glassblowers made to amuse themselves or test their skill, for giving to friends perhaps or to sell and make a little extra for their pay-packets, and the commercially made trifles of the Victorian age is very thin. Probably only the expert can help here. I saw recently a blown-glass horse on a square base made of a thin tube of glass which was marked Nailsea. In fact I had often bought similar ones, manufactured in

Nevers spun-glass crèche made at the end of the 18th
century. The brilliant colours are very beautiful.
(*Courtesy of the Musée des Arts Décoratifs, Paris*)

the 1930's in Czechoslovakia, for 6d. each at Woolworth's. Very
good they were, provided no one was trying to sell them as antiques.
In fact old glass animals never seem to be set on a tubular base.

Early glass bells date from about 1755, some made from bottle
glass of fairly crude workmanship. These were probably made by
experimentally minded apprentice boys, like the pieces described
three quarters of a century later by Apsley Pellatt. Bristol glassmakers produced a fascinating variety of gloriously coloured glass
bells in red, emerald or white opaque glass. Some of the handles
were of flint glass with knops or decorated with exquisite enamel
twists of gay colours. Then there were enormous tobacco pipes
with multi-knopped stems, though their outsize really forbids
their appearance in a book on miniatures. Cigarette or cigar-
holders, with a bird perched on the stem, are admissible, of course,
and possibly the glass rollers. These were first of all simply salt

containers and made of dark bottle glass. For centuries consecrated salt was believed to be a sure charm against witchcraft or the evil eye, and when they were later on found to be extremely handy for rolling pastry, they were blown with straight sides, instead of the early elliptical air-tight shape, with both ends knobbed. The Bristol and Nailsea, Newcastle, Sunderland and London rollers were most of them made by glassworkers in their spare time. They are clear glass or pale blue or green. At first they were enamelled and then painted in coloured oil paints and lightly fired. Afterwards came the transfer decorations in the mid-19th century. As all the glassworks that made them were near the coast, presumably their sale was largely to sailors, who gave them as parting presents to wives or sweethearts. We find them with touching inscriptions like 'This roller round it is for you, If you'll be constant, I'll be true'. There are frequent drawings of ships, and others are made of pretty opaque white glass, which may be striped or flecked with different colours.

Canes, shepherds' crooks and walking sticks, coming from the same glassworks, were made both for hanging decoratively in the best parlour, and for carrying in processions, when the makers displayed their wonderfully contrived, delicate and colourful pieces. These, like so many other of their lesser works, were probably considered as bringers of good fortune. As with the rollers, the earliest walking-sticks which were tapered and twisted ones, were made from the pale green bottle glass, whilst the next in date are gay colours such as red, yellow, green, blue and opaque white, with ribbons of enamel or spirals, also in colour, inset. There are some with cut diamond designs on them and they come in any size between four and eight feet long. How sparkling they must have looked in the Processions of their exhibits. Accounts in newspapers of the early 19th century describe such wonders as a glass fort carrying seven glass cannons which actually fired salutes; a Chinese pagoda with a chime of bells; a glass windmill with its sails in motion and a musical accompaniment from instruments made of glass like hunting horns, bugles and bells. The tunes were probably not very complicated, as glass instruments cannot be fitted up with valves. The total amount of notes they achieve is only four. However, the ingenuity and skill of the glassblowers, wearing glass insignia and woven glass plumes on their helmets, must have been a sight for sore eyes. There were swords, too, whose blades had twisted spirals of coloured glass inside them, whilst others were made of light blue glass with realistic bloody tips of scarlet. The polehead emblems of village friendly societies are usually of brass, but there were apparently a few made of glass, notably for the Nailsea Glassmakers' Guild.

III

A Miscellany

With maddening frequency we are told that anything big related to the home has been made in miniature size, and indeed that is probably as nearly true as makes no difference. Those lovely Dutch 'cabinets' and the baby houses of the past were given every luxury their contemporaries could make. Small milk-glass tea sets date, however, to the early 19th century and so do the charming striped jugs of the same glass. The glass domes, known to the Victorians as 'shades', figure in various tiny sizes for dolls' houses, to cover little wax figurines and minute ornaments but especially clocks. There are glass chandeliers and gas or electric lighting shades, some of Bristol glass. These are to be found in many designs, and there are little mirrors too, most of them gilt-framed and chiefly of Victorian date. Although there are many modern decanters, wine glasses and tumblers, there are also amusing Victorian goblets and jugs with embossed 'pewter' settings. The Bristol Museum shows enchanting wine glasses with coloured twists in the stems. There are even examples of miniscule cut-glass sets for the dinner-table.

The Queen's Dolls' House at Windsor has of course decanters just over an inch high and glasses half the size, but of course these are modern. The wine cellar is right to the last detail too, as was to be expected. However, it will not be in our lifetime that this remarkable dolls' house can be classified as antique, so we must leave it for the present un-sung, except briefly.

The fabulous French, English and American glass paper-weights are so fully documented that it is best to leave this specialist subject to the expert and simply mention two or three of the humbler glass weights which are not so often mentioned. There are, for instance, those delightful bottle-green glass doorstops with

Three miniature glass candle sticks, in clean and brilliant blue glass—early 19th century.

imprisoned flowers, fountains or bubbles and sometimes figures, in humble imitation of the great Apsley Pellatt's sulphides. Cristallo-céramie was the name of the French process, inspired by Bohemian glass of the 1750's, and Apsley Pellatt made it to perfection in this country from 1821 in his glasshouse at Southwark. He not only made glass incrustations for paperweights but used this form of decoration for wine decanters and glasses, toilet flasks and other pieces, having taken out a patent for their manufacture. This did not prevent the later production of fairground types of paper-weights being made with incrustations, like the bottle-green doorstops, which sometimes have pottery ware angels or other figures in them, though not nearly as elegant and charming as the delicate flowers in their pots. Another constant worry for collectors is the way reproductions appear in so many fields, and unfortunately there are modern 'dumps' or doorstops, though they are not difficult to detect in comparison with an old one. It is comforting how one reproduction placed amongst a collection of old things gives itself away.

I have an amusing example of a painted lion's head contained in a clear glass paperweight, of which I have never seen another example. It must be Victorian.

The French factories made exquisite sulphides, of course, and Baccarat, in the mid-19th century, produced cameos of Queen Victoria and other famous people incrusted in clear glass, as well as a splendid figure of Joan of Arc and sometimes mythological figures or sporting scenes. They are still producing these today at Baccarat, including portraits of famous men of the past and also Eisenhower, our Queen Elizabeth and Sir Winston Churchill.

It is therefore perhaps safer for the less experienced collector to try the field that is not either so full of hazards or so competitive. Victorian scenes from coloured prints were fixed on to the bottom of clear glass paperweights from about the time of the Great Exhibition in 1851. There may be some earlier in the 1840's and they were also made on the Continent with charming street scenes or views of popular places. Views of the Crystal Palace when it was in Hyde Park must have done quite a roaring trade at the time and these often have little scraps of tinsel behind the great glass windows, giving the sparkling effect of the sun shining on the glass. The weights made after about 1890 are less interesting as they were then debased by using photographic views, most of which have faded like old photographs in the albums of the time. However, it is as well to remember that after much research Mr. Geoffrey A. Godden[1] discovered that before, and presumably up to 1937 glass was imported from abroad, or prints were sent to be stuck on the glass; so they continued to be popular well into the 20th century.

There are not only round scenic weights to be found, but in the last quarter of the 19th century we may find square, oblong, fluted and even heart-shaped weights, and probably the best tip for collectors would be to try to concentrate as far as possible on the great varieties of interesting scenes up to 1890.

Sadly these little weights seldom have labels to tell us where or

[1] *Antique China and Glass under £5* by Geoffrey A. Godden, 1966.

88

by whom they were made. Since Mr. Godden's book including useful information about them appeared, they have found their place amongst collectors' items.

IV

Some Bottles, Flasks and Ornaments

Bristol is famous not only for its magnificent dark blue glass, but also for the exquisite opaque white glass which is decorated in enamel colours. There is so little of this porcelain-like dense, creamy white glass for collectors to find, decorated by Michael Edkins from 1762 to 1787[1], and also by his son and probably others too, that we can only look longingly in museums, at examples of this 18th century glass, unless our pockets are very well lined.

Opaque white glass was invented at least two thousand years ago in Egypt, but the art was then lost until the Venetians revived it at the end of the 16th century. Bristol's 18th century opaque white glass was quite different from that produced elsewhere and apparently the Redcliffe Backs Glasshouse first made it in this high quality. In those days it was called enamel glass, or 'white and painted enamel glass'. This early glass had a punty-mark on the base of each piece, which was later ground off at the factories.

Tapersticks, six or seven inches high, like miniature candlesticks, cruet bottles, vases, small tea-caddies about five or six inches high, mugs, basins and jars and scent bottles were all decorated with sprays of flowers or butterflies, birds and wreaths of leaves or even imitation Chinese figures. Sometimes the name of the owner is inscribed on them with the date. There are examples in the Victoria and Albert Museum, including at least one from that fabulous collection made by Lady Charlotte Schreiber, most of which was of porcelain and pottery. It is always useful to look at authentic specimens in museums. In this case once you have seen the Bristol enamel glass you will never confuse it with the milk-white glass made in other places.

Toilet bottles in Bristol blue glass, decorated with enamel and mounted in gold, give an appearance of great beauty and richness. There are also beautiful smelling bottles and scent bottles designed

---

[1] *The Collectors' Dictionary of Glass* by E. M. Elville. 1961.

by Apsley Pellatt (1791–1863) and crystallo-céramie examples too, such as the one inset with a portrait of the ill-fated Princess Charlotte, daughter of the Prince Regent. All of these lovely pieces are greatly sought after of course.

Nailsea is a term given to a troup of fascinating glass bottles, jugs and other wares, striped, looped or flecked with coloured enamels and now it is obvious that a good deal of what was classified as 'Nailsea' in fact came from other centres as well, like Stourbridge, Bristol, Alloa and St. Helens, Tyneside, Warrington, Yorkshire and Wrockwardine. So we are saddled with the designation of 'Nailsea', but must look upon it merely as the name of a style and not the specific factory from which the wares came. Experts say that the jugs with splashes of colour on them, including the more generally found white splashes, come from both Sunderland and Shropshire, whilst from Wrockwardine in Shropshire come the bottles with the yellow mottling which we find on some flecked examples.

One of the most attractive bottles from this type of glass is the gimmel flask, either with one neck, or made, like some oil-and-vinegar bottles, with two necks. They may have white enamel festoons on clear glass, opaque white glass with red and blue festoons and other variations. They range in size from three and a half to ten and a half inches high. Scent and toilet water bottles in Nailsea style are very attractive and come in many shapes and colours. They were sometimes made to resemble a hairdresser's bellows for whitening his customers' wigs or hair. Much later, in the mid-1870's, Sowerby advertised his 'Patent Queen's Ivory Ware' with its crest trade mark of which I have an example. It is a wall-pocket in the shape of a bellows, with little Jack Horner impressed on one side. This was representing a fireside bellows, however, and not the hairdressers' version.

All this coloured glass came to enrich our homes from about 1815. It included a regiment of different wares from jars and vases to butter boats with handles and hats for toothpicks, toddy-lifters, egg-cups and everything needed for the dressing-table, the dining-table and the nursery. Those delightful Christmas lights, decorated with a close diamond pattern, were blown in moulds from many different coloured transparent pot metals; and in the second half of the 19th century came the coloured glass night-lights made popular by Samuel Clarke, who was incidentally a past master in the art of advertising.

Once we reach what a fellow-writer called 'the Victorian Maze', there is no end to the variety and scope for glass collectors.

MINIATURE JEWELLERY AND SMALL BOXES

I

Jewellery

Personal adornment must have a history nearly as old as food. When we go to the Zoo and look rather uneasily at our nearest animal relative the ape and offer him a piece of cloth or ribbon he invariably sniffs it first to see if it is edible and then tries it for size on his head. Flowers must always have played a great part in dressing up and children make daisy-chains for necklaces to this day; that is if they can find them in our weed-deprived lawns.

Precious stones were highly valued in ancient civilizations. In biblical times the breast plate of the High Priest was decorated with twelve gems of inestimable value, on each of which was engraved the name of one of the tribes of Israel. In the Talmud a charming legend tells how Noah lit his ark by the light of precious stones. Apparently Abraham jealously kept all his wives shut up in a city where a lordly dish was filled with precious stones to illuminate the whole place by night and by day. The walls were built too high to admit either sun, moon or starlight.

In Nero's golden palace the panels of the rooms were made out of mother-of-pearl and encrusted with gold and gems. As for that cruelly mad Emperor Caligula's wife, she is described by Pliny as being covered with emeralds and pearls on her head, neck, arms and girdle. She seems to have been more interested in the price of her jewels however than in their beauty. Pliny reports that 'their value she was prepared to prove on the instant by producing the receipts.'.

Agnés Sorel (1422–50), mistress of Charles VII of France, is said to have made diamonds fashionable in France. She was called *La Dame de Beauté* both for her personal charms and because her royal lover gave her the *seigneurie* of Beauté-sur-Marne near Vincennes. Diamonds used to be thought to have power against poisons, plagues, sorcery, insanity and evil spirits. They were also given credit for being able to safeguard virtue. The sure test of a wife's fidelity was to slip a diamond under her pillow without her knowledge, when her dreams would betray the state of her heart, 'and she mutters in her unrest a name she dare not breathe by day.'.

The height of extravagance in Europe seems to have been reached in the reigns of Louis XIII and Louis XIV. The conquests of Mexico and Peru towards the end of the 16th century led to the discovery of rich mines of precious metals. The noblemen very often sewed all their family diamonds, pearls and other jewels on their clothes and in England James I's favourite, the Duke of Buckingham, had a court suit worth a small fortune on which the diamonds were purposely sewn on loosely so that they might fall off and cause the ladies of the Court to compete for them in an ungainly scramble.

The French Revolution put a stop to all this wild extravagance particularly in France. Presumably many aristocrats managed to hide or carry away some of their family jewels, but the *citoyens* and *citoyennes* displayed only a few poor trinkets which were shaped in propaganda emblems like the bunch of faggots of fasces, caps of liberty, triangles and even guillotines. The period of the Directoire (1795–9), overthrown by Bonaparte, saw a fashion revived for wearing rings on the toes. Fashionable ladies promenaded in Roman sandals showing off their be-gemmed feet. Slowly the jewellers' art revived again under Napoleon, with plain rings and coral beads, cameos and pearls in pseudo-antique taste. Then came the Restoration and diamonds were fashionable again, though in France the nobility had so few of their family heirlooms left, that semi-precious coloured stones had to be called into service.

However, with the advent of the 1851 Exhibition there were many lovely pieces of good quality on show, including a priceless black diamond, weighing 350 carats, which was too hard to polish.

Most collectors today are likely to find that Victorian and Edwardian jewellery will fit both their taste and their purses, as the earlier pieces are mostly in the millionaire class. An article written in 1865 bears witness to the contemporary interest in rubies,

93

sapphires and emeralds. Apparently an emerald, worn as an amulet around the neck, possesses many of the metaphysical properties of the diamond. It puts evil spirits to flight, guards the wearer against epilepsy and is also a preserver of chastity. What a pleasant thought that our beautiful jewels have this satisfactory control over the powers of darkness.

The mid-Victorian period from say 1860 to about 1885 is a particularly rich one to explore. The pieces are large and beautifully coloured and much less delicate and fragile than those of the earlier more romantic period. For one thing, women were beginning to venture out of their homes into the worlds of politics and even business and in 1873 a landmark was reached when three girls passed the Cambridge Tripos. Consequently women had money to spend and much of it went on the magnificently flamboyant necklaces and earrings, brooches and bracelets inspired by the classical revival style of jewellery made popular by the famous Italian jeweller Augusto Castellani, the brilliant son of a remarkable father who founded the business. His brother Alessandro, by the way, gathered together a fabulous collection of ancient jewellery which is now in the care of the British Museum.

These Etruscan and Greek reproductions of ancient ornaments were extremely popular, and their technical merit was outstanding. Names to remember of other jewellers of this period are Carlo Giuliano and his sons Federico and Fernando, who settled in London, having originally come from Naples; Robert Phillips, who was one of our best designers, and John Brogden, who made jewellery inspired by the Eastern cultures of Egypt, Abyssinia and China.

British designers also were inspired by their own traditions of the Anglo-Saxons and Celts and they used agate and marble pebbles and topaz, mostly in a setting of silver.

'Scotch jewellery', says my copy of *The Englishwoman's Domestic Magazine* of 1867, 'is *de rigueur*'. Apparently badges of different clans, regardless of whether the wearers belonged to them, were worn as 'brooches, earrings, buckles and as the centre of shoe-rosettes.'

The Italian influence brought us enamelled miniatures and mosaics set in jet, both as brooches and necklaces. When Queen Victoria became Empress of India in 1876 it is not much of a surprise to find imitations of Indian jewellery becoming fashionable. A necklace of seed pearls and moonstone drops is a personally cherished heirloom, lovely to look at but not of great worth. Motifs of the period included birds, beasts, serpents, insects and roses, lotus-flowers and shells, with the best settings made out of gold in different shades and using such stones as diamonds, emeralds, pearls, rubies and sapphires, amethyst, turquoise and opal.

Silver also was used as well as onyx, enamel, coral and malachite. Pebble jewellery, mostly agate, was in the less expensive class of ornament, and steel and tortoiseshell, either plain or in pretty piqué designs, was much in evidence. Ivory was used in brooches, usually carved into flowers, but also it was formed into crosses and anchors. The crosses were also made of gold or silver elaborately set with diamonds, rubies, emeralds, or less expensively with coral, turquoise or pearls and they were sometimes enamelled. The shape of the crosses might be either Greek, Latin, Irish or Maltese.

The Victorians were very fond of the strange and bizarre so that fanciful gold brooches can be found set with jewels, representing a deaths' head, a champagne bottle, a pipe or a half-open golden pod of pearl peas. Tigers' claws set in gold were much admired and these were also set less richly in silver and their date is circa 1870–5. A fantastic parure of these sinister decorative motifs had a necklace of twelve claws mounted in gold flower and leaf settings, a pair of claws hanging on three chains as earrings and a brooch of two claws mounted by a small gold tiger. The bracelet comprised eight similarly mounted claws. In my Victorian collection is a beautifully made vinaigrette mounted on a tiger's claw and a second-class type of brooch with two claws bound together in chased silver. They are not my favourite pieces, but probably appeal to those who are attracted by the unusual. The mid-Victorian ladies liked their jewellery to represent anything from walnuts to coal scuttles, from dogs and horses to ladders and locomotives and from violets to horseshoes. Nothing was too outrageous to please their fancy and sporting jewellery, much admired by Napoleon III, was another passing vogue of this period.

The most peculiar fashion perhaps was for insects. These were featured not only on necklaces, earrings and bracelets but

Two lace or tie pins. The serpent coiled into a knot is
c. 1845 and made of chased gold. The dog's head is set in
silver with diamond eyes.

also on parasols, veils and bonnets. Flies, beetles, butterflies, bees
and dragonflies all appeared either in brightly coloured enamels
or captured under crystal domes on brooches, earrings or pins.

   Those with less exotic tastes might prefer to collect early Victorian
jewellery, with its romantic interest in the Middle Ages and the
Renaissance. Here such names as François-Desiré Froment-
Meurice and Rudolphi, both from Paris, were notable designers.
Seed-pearls, coral turquoise, mosaics, cameos and strange jewellery
made of fossils were characteristic of the early Victorian taste,
when the 'jewellery of sentiment' was so popular. Amateurs and
professionals made lockets, brooches and earrings of human hair;

This pendant-brooch is *c.* 1860–80 with jewelled
enamel and pearl drops showing a Renaissance influence.

exquisite little landscapes some of them were, and flower designs
and elegant bunches of hair and feathers caught in gold ribbons too.

Probably on account of the Crimean War and also the Indian
Mutiny, many pieces of mourning jewellery were made and jet
was much used. Of course the death of William IV and then later
of the Prince Consort must have added to the number of sombre
pieces of jewellery required.

Lava was another unusual material which was carved into designs
and set in pinchbeck or silver for bracelets, earrings and necklaces;
nor was horsehair left out, for we can find many bracelets, rings
and plaited brooches made of this seemingly uninspiring substance

97

and bog-oak from Ireland was also pressed into service. The Victorians were filled with adventurous and enterprising notions; and of course this was the great period for work done by innumerable ladies of leisure, who occupied their spare time, encouraged by magazines bursting with good ideas, in making all sorts of curiously touching absurdities like slippers galore from beads and Berlin wool; velvet 'toilet cushions' which you and I would crudely call footstools; watch-hooks, watch-pockets, carriage footwarmers, mats, albums, pictures, the lot. All these painstakingly made knick-knacks are avidly collected today in an age when practically nothing is made by hand.

Art Nouveau jewellery of about 1880–1910 has a strange appeal which, in its less exotic form, many of us have felt. An exquisite necklet of moonstones set in an open silver mount ornamented with enamel and linked with twisted gold wire was designed by Hugh Seebohm in the late 1890's and the work carried out by C. R. Ashbee, who also designed jewellery himself. Huge baroque pearls were often used most effectively and 'pearl blisters' might be set in enamel. Pendants were very much liked and the strange botanical shapes of Art Nouveau translated into jewellery at its best is bewitchingly beautiful.

Enamelling is a very ancient art and in Egypt the glassmakers used enamel to glaze their tiles and pottery at least a thousand years before Christ. For use in jewellery enamelling dates back to about 500 B.C. and some of our museums have examples both of our own Celtic work and Egyptian and Classical Roman and Greek brooches and pendants. As for the famous pieces in the Victoria and Albert Museum, like the late-18th century Venetian Ship pendant, the Italian late-16th century 'Canning Jewel', where a curiously shaped pearl has been used as a man's body; these show where the Art Nouveau artists like Alexander Fisher and Harold Stapler and others, found such inspiration for their own work. Fabergé's exquisite and costly inspirations make great use of enamel too.

Temptations are alluringly set out to trap collectors into buying more than they intended, and as always it is so important to choose the best of its kind. A good dealer and a good book help beginners and old hands alike. The expensive but discriminating purchase of today may turn into the bargain of tomorrow; but the bargain of today could well disappoint us tomorrow. Experience, Oscar Wilde remarked, is the name people give to their mistakes. Yes, and mistakes can be very dear sometimes. All the same, in the long run experience is our best teacher.

II
Snuff-Boxes

So many of these little necessaries of the 18th century fashionable life were made of rare and precious materials, at least in their hey-day, that they are included under jewellery.

Miniature representations of every day things seem to have attracted most craftsmen. For instance, in the form of shoes or boots we can find snuff-boxes, vinaigrettes, nutmeg graters, match-containers and signets for a start. A great many of the snuff-box shoes were made of wood and the carved ones are in styles ranging from mediaeval days right up to the end of the 19th century. In fact, as snuff was not introduced into Europe until the late 16th century, and we English were not really addicted to the habit until the 18th century, those mediaeval shoes were probably most of them made in the early days of Queen Victoria, when a passion for the Middle Ages affected fashions in all the arts.

Snuff was taken in England during the plague of 1614, and later in the more famous plague of 1665, when it was a recognised antidote recommended by doctors. Soon people began to enjoy it in every day life and not just when the plague was a menace. They even used walking-sticks fitted with snuff-boxes in the handles. This was a convenient way of taking a pinch during their walks abroad. The handles of walking sticks and parasols were made in all sorts of amusing shapes like alligators, monkey, ass, human and bulldog heads, and 17th century sticks may be topped with grotesque heads, satyrs, puttis and other fantastic shapes. John Wesley has appeared as the handle of a walking stick and many of the animal heads carved in wood had moveable ears or jaws. How-ever, this is a digression and we will return to this entertaining subject in another chapter.

Shoe snuff-boxes made out of wood were believed to be *tours-de-force* of cobblers' apprentices when they graduated from their masters' workshops to set up on their own. This may well be true of the delightful models, studded with brass tacks, often with the date or a lovers' emblem like entwined hearts or the sweetheart's name marked on the sole or the lid in nails. Sometimes they were inlaid with ivory or mother-of-pearl. They were also made in pairs or even joined together with two separate lids. Some of the shoe snuff-boxes are six or seven inches long, when of course they would not be carried in the pocket but set on the table to share with friends. Snuff-box shoes are found in horn, brass, pewter, papier-mâché and even porcelain and enamel.

A description of the variety of snuff-box shapes would fill a book. Table snuff-boxes, even the very high quality gold and silver ones, do not belong in this book due to their size; but pocket ones can be found in such macabre shapes as coffins, which are a sad memento mori of a dead friend, or skulls. They also appear in the shape of books, Napoleonic hats and helmets, goldfinches and pugs, and fish heads of Bilston and French enamel, as well as human heads. They are carved from Coquilla nuts, which are German or Dutch in origin, and these are shaped as tortoises, toads, boars' heads, dogs' heads, pigs, fishes, monkeys and sometimes grotesque little human figures with glass eyes. No wonder snuff-boxes in all these miscellaneous shapes are so much sought after, for they satisfy the child in us all just as much as true toys do.

An essential for any snuff-box was a very tight and well-fitting lid. The table snuff-boxes often had detachable lids, but the pocket ones mostly had hinged lids to make them close tightly.

Ordinary plain boxes sound comparatively dull after all this variety in cheaper materials, but there is quite a diversity in the more conventional shapes. For example, there were straw-work snuff-boxes, which were made in France from about 1750. Souvenir or tourist boxes of the 18th century were made from tortoiseshell, from rock-salt in Spain and oddest of all, from coal. In 1766 Horace Walpole ordered some 'coal' snuff-boxes to be sent to the wife of the French Ambassador to England. They were apparently highly polished to look like black marble. Could they in fact have been jet, perhaps, which is a mineralized and fossilized product like coal? Jet has been used since at least 2000 B.C. in Britain for adornment. Lava from Vesuvius was also made into snuff-boxes for travellers to take home as souvenirs.

Best of all these little boxes were the really exquisite miniature works of art that were made from about the time when the word 'snuff-box' was first used, which was apparently in 1681. Of course collectors need to have a bottomless purse to buy this quality of box. For one thing they were not only made of gold, silver or enamel, but they were often encrusted with pearls or diamonds.

The ceremony of taking snuff from one of these elegant little boxes became an elaborate fashionable ritual, and early gold snuff-boxes, together with ones for sweetmeats, patches and pounce, more or less indistinguishable from each other in those days, would have been found on all fashionable dressing tables.

Oval boxes were most common in England at the end of the 17th century until about 1780, and then the shape changed to oblong. But there were many charming shell-shaped boxes and ones made from the actual shells, cowries, mussels and so forth. French ladies might possess, like the Duchesse d'Orléans, quite a collection of boxes of gold and porcelain and enamel, all of which were imitated in England.

Boxes now fetching large prices were enamelled ones made in the shapes of animals, birds and shoes or representing sedan-chairs, boats, hearts and books, and other fanciful forms. There are display cases full of these enchanting snuff-boxes at the *Musée des Arts Décoratifs* in Paris and at the Wallace Collection in London, the Victoria and Albert Museum and a great many other places. They have never lost favour with collectors.

For some unexplained reason a small box has always had an irresistible appeal for every age and sex, since time immemorial. Offer anybody a box to look at and his immediate reaction will be to open it and look inside. What do we expect to find? Hidden treasure, perhaps. Sometimes we are lucky. A small Tunbridge-ware snuff-box I found recently had a tiny painted metal *folie-bergère* figure inside, whose arms and legs flutter at the slightest movement. Oddly enough the seller had not, in this instance, opened the box, which goes to show that the instinct always to open one must be a wise impulse.

The aristocratic snuff-boxes of silver and gold, hardstone and metal, enamel, Meissen porcelain and tortoiseshell *piqué*, ones decorated with mother-of-pearl, ornamental engravings, miniature landscape paintings or portraits, enamelled or set with diamonds or pearls are enchantingly lovely. The really fashionable man of taste would have had at least as many snuff-boxes as he had costumes in the mid-18th century. When Boswell attended the sale of Count Heinrich von Brühl's possessions in 1764 he noted 'upwards of seven hundred snuff-boxes in gold and many of them very rich with diamonds.'.

Paris craftsmen combined Sèvres porcelain with diamonds, but this would have been only for a chosen few. Our own silversmith Matthew Boulton, who was born in 1728 and lived to a ripe eighty-one years old, was producing 'toys and utensils of various kinds, in gold, copper, tortoiseshell and enamels . . .' catering from about 1768 for all tastes. His factory was in Soho. The 'toys' probably included ormolu and tortoiseshell and agate snuff-boxes though attribution is difficult as the boxes were not marked, unless they were silver and not always even then. In France on the other hand all silver and gold boxes were marked. Now came the time that Boulton and his colleagues were most likely also producing the many snuff-boxes available in enamel making use of transfer printing and using steel and papier-mâché. This of course put snuff-boxes in the reach of everybody. Gone were the days when gold snuff-boxes were offered as gifts by royalty as a mark of their favour, which was a custom that had been current in France from about 1668. Beau Nash was given a 'very fine snuff-box' by the Prince of Orange. This gesture developed into a fashion, so that Mr. Nash must have been quite overwhelmed by these expensive 'toys' being showered upon him by the nobility and by 'the middling gentry', who soon followed suit.

A melancholy story that is quite unexpected in connection with such little masterpieces as these exquisite gold snuff-boxes, is the melting down of a considerable number of George IV's own gold boxes. Very few of these lovely little snuff-boxes exist because so many were broken up in the first quarter of the 19th century, the diamonds being re-set and the gold made up into some other more fashionable trinket. The fashion for them seems to have died with Napoleon, he having had no less than one hundred gold portrait boxes made in 1806, presumably as gifts to give to political supporters.[1]

[1] Those interested in a full history of the more luxurious European snuff-boxes should read *European and American Snuff-Boxes 1730–1830*, by Claire Corbeiller. B. T. Batsford Ltd., 1966.

III
Vinaigrettes

Patch boxes, sweetmeat boxes, nutmeg graters and vinaigrettes all come under the category of miniature antiques and probably the most popular, as they are at present fairly reasonable in price, are vinaigrettes. These, as well as nutmeg graters, are easier to distinguish as to their special purpose than those intended for snuff, patches, sweetmeats, or even counters. Vinaigrettes were made in every bit as wide a variety of shapes and materials as snuff-boxes and their particular beauty is the grille which covers the tiny sponge soaked in aromatic vinegar inside the little box. Gold and silversmiths went to great lengths to decorate the grilles in attractive patterns, as well of course as the lids. Birmingham has been associated with the making of small boxes in precious metals since the 17th century,[1] and the names of such masters as the Pemberton family; the several Matthew Linwoods; the Mills family, of whom Joseph Mills was the founder of the firm; the Willmores and Joseph Taylor all worked in Birmingham. Another famous name is Matthew Boulton, though Mr. Delieb points out that he was not actually a silversmith himself, but the power behind a successful firm. Anyone wishing to specialize in the collection of silver or gold boxes should provide himself with a copy of Mr. Delieb's book (see note below), which is a mine of carefully researched information as well as brilliantly illustrated.

In early days it was fashionable to carry a pomander the ancestor of the vinaigrette, to guard against infections and keep evil smells at bay. Originally an orange stuck with cloves or the pulp taken out and the skin filled with a sponge soaked in sweet-scented vinegar, was carried by the more fastidious, and this habit went on well into the 18th century. However, Henry VIII preferred a pouncet box of gold or silver encrusted with jewels and fitted with a sponge soaked in vinegar. This was made from sage and rosemary, lavender, cloves and other delicious spices all mixed with alcohol and camphor after having been left soaking for two weeks and then the liquid sieved on to the sponge. Pouncet merely means perforated, and the word pounce box later on referred to the

---

[1] *Silver Boxes* by Eric Delieb. Herbert Jenkins, 1968.

dredger for scattering sand on ink to dry it before the invention of blotting paper. However, in Shakespeare's Henry IV a dandified nobleman, obviously much scorned by the dramatist, is described by Hotspur as being 'perfumed like a milliner; and 'twixt his finger and his thumb he held a pouncet-box, which ever and anon he gave his nose and took it away again.' Henry VIII and his courtiers had pouncet-boxes conveniently set into their walking sticks, or they hung them round their waists by a cord. Later, from about 1830, they often hung from chatelaines, together with scissors, a thimble and a notebook and pencil, or else they were fitted with a ring for hanging on the fob or on a simple chain.

Pouncet boxes and later so-called sponge boxes did not have the elaborate grilles, so much desired by collectors today. They had simple perforations. However, in about 1770 aromatic vinegar was made so strong and potent with concentrated oils that 'the elegant gold aromatic box' became conveniently much smaller. Later still in the 1820's an even stronger vinegar was used and all silver vinaigrettes were gilded inside to prevent the acid from attacking the more vulnerable silver.

The grilles or grids have such patterns as cornucopias of fruit, flowers and leaves, birds, and even fishes. Sometimes they are pierced with the owners coat of arms. Victorian grilles are sometimes uninteresting dull ones with crosses, concentric circle or oblongs. The little boxes themselves are quite irresistible in their multitude of amusing shapes. There are early Victorian flexible fishes with garnet eyes; the very popular press-embossed pictures of well-known buildings like Windsor Castle, St. Paul's Cathedral or fashionable stately homes. Some are shaped like shells or hearts, books, watches and after about 1820 they are set with agate, onyx and other semi-precious stones. The Victorian cast rose-bud with a leaf and smaller bud on the stalk was made by Edward H. Stockwell in London in 1888. It is shown in Mr. Delieb's *Investing in Silver* and apparently the lid is a hinged petal concealed on the top of the flower. The silver vinaigrettes marked fully with the famous names already mentioned are very desirable and much collected.

MINIATURE PORTRAITS

I

Miniatures

John Smart (1741 ?–1811), one of our best 18th century miniaturists, first exhibited in 1762. Master miniaturists generally signed their work and Smart almost always signed his with his initials. However it is often extremely difficult to discover them and necessitates removing the picture from its setting. The initials will sometimes be found very close to the edge of the ivory. Looking for signatures in any miniature is quite a puzzle and it is advisable to search for the microscopic initials, sometimes in monogram and occasionally in gold, hidden in draperies or in the curls of the wig or the lady's hair. Often they are only visible in a particular angle of light.

Another fashionable painter in his day, was Sir William Charles Ross, born in London in 1794. He is often said to be the last really great miniature painter of the 19th century. His father, William Ross, was a successful Scottish miniaturist. He received recognition no less than seven times from the Society of Arts and painted Queen Victoria and the Prince Consort as well as Napoleon III and the King and Queen of the Belgians and the sovereigns of Portugal. He charged 17 guineas for his smallest size, the next 'larger without hands' cost 25 guineas and 'the largest which includes the hands' 35 guineas.

English miniature painting started, to all intents and purposes, when Holbein, to escape religious intolerance, came on his first visit to England in 1526, carrying an introduction to Sir Thomas More, given to him by his patron Erasmus. He painted the More family and also some of their rich and important friends and then returned, after two very successful years, to Basle; but still the city was a hotbed of religious dissention, so in 1532 he returned again to England.

There are very few miniatures in existence today that were

A beautiful miniature signed by John Smart and dated 1776. The lady wears a pale green dress under a red fur-trimmed cloak. The frame is bordered in diamonds.
(*Courtesy of Sotheby & Co.*)

undoubtedly by Holbein, so many were copied; but the Royal collections at Windsor Castle and elsewhere have several authentic portraits, including ones of Catherine Howard[1] and the Duke of Suffolk's two sons. These last were both painted on the backs of playing-cards, which was apparently a surface that miniaturists liked to paint on, because it was so smooth. They were called tables and Hilliard referred to them as 'smooth as any satine.' Here is not the place to consider all the learnéd discussions that have excited scholars for years over the authenticity of many miniatures ascribed to Holbein. His mastery over the art of portraiture, both full-size and in miniature, is quite outstanding and his insight into the characters of his models, the finesse in every delicate jewel, embroidery and even the hair or the beard, all show the technique of a genius. Of course miniature portraits were hung or pinned on to clothes as ornaments from Holbein's day until the end of the 18th century.

After his day many foreign painters continued to come to England and were patronized by the sovereign, but in Elizabeth's reign our first and noteworthy English miniaturist Nicholas Hilliard took up his artist's profession from an early age, having started work as a goldsmith. He was soon appointed portrait

[1]This one was also copied; possibly by Isaac Oliver.

This 'most exquisitely painted water colour' by Peter Oliver shows that man of many parts, Sir Kenelm Digby (1603–1665), wearing a white lace Van Dyck collar over a gold embroidered doublet. This miniature fetched £1550 in a sale at Sotheby's in May, 1971.
(Courtesy of Sotheby & Co.)

painter to the Queen. He often used a pale blue background and always arranged his sitter in the circle or oval with a conspicuous sense of design and composition. Sadly his colours have faded, especially the flesh-tints. But his elaborate treatment of jewellery, lace and embroideries make his portraits resemble some of the old illuminators in the flatness of the treatment, though in fact it was Holbein whom he admired and on whom he modelled his own work.

Isaac Oliver, and his son Peter, next take the stage. Isaac studied under Hilliard as well as under the Italian Zucchero. He painted a number of very excellent large miniatures, one being the splendid portrait of Sir Philip Sidney under a tree, full of exquisite and delicate details. The two Olivers and Hilliard are always associated together in this the first period of English miniature portrait painting.

Isaac's son Peter was taught by his father and he was patronized by Charles I who gave him the job of copying in water colour some of his best liked pictures at Whitehall. In this way the King was able to carry them with him and enjoy looking at them when he was away from home. Charles I was a passionate connoisseur, a dedicated collector with a genuine taste and love for all kinds of art in an Age when one country ruthlessly plundered another during wars and carried off priceless national treasures to add prestige to their own art collections.

The seventeenth century is generally supposed to be the greatest time in the art of portrait painting in England. The man whose name is one of the best known and some say the best miniaturist of any age, was the brilliant Samuel Cooper. He was taught by his Uncle John Hoskins, who died in 1664. It is said that Hoskins signed and dated all his portraits, and in some cases one can see that eventually the uncle was influenced by his nephew-pupil's work. Cooper has been described as 'the English Vandyck', and certainly he studied and admired the Dutch painter. He really belongs to the Commonwealth period and he painted many illustrious men and women before he died in 1672. One of his most famous miniatures was of Oliver Cromwell, and other splendid examples of his work shows Charles II, James II, John Milton and 'La Belle Stuart'.

The diarist John Evelyn was commanded to come to King Charles II's closet one January evening in 1662 and found 'Mr. Cooper, the rare limner, crayonning of the King's face and head, to make the stamps by for the new milled money now contriving. I had the honour to hold the candle whilst it was doing, he choosing the night and candle-light for the better finding out the shadows.'[1]

Sir Peter Lely, the famous portrait painter of the Restoration, had many pupils and amongst them was Thomas Flatman (1637–88) who was an artist of considerable gifts, and considered to be second only to Cooper. Another accomplished pupil was Nathaniel Dixon who painted the scheming Louise de Kéroal,[2] Duchess of Portsmouth.

Up to the end of the 17th century water-colour and gouache miniatures were painted on card or vellum, whilst oil paintings

[1] Evelyn's *Diary*.
[2] Spelling given by Larousse.

108

A miniature of a gentleman by Richard Cosway, signed and dated in full. He wears a white waistcoat and cravat under a blue jacket and his hair is powdered.
(*Courtesy of Sotheby & Co.*)

were on panel, slate, copper and even silver occasionally. Now the new base was ivory, and gradually it supplanted all other bases for water colour.

The 18th century saw a great change of style as, by the end of the 17th century with the indolent and sensuous Court of Charles II, portraits became less realistic and dignified and more pandering to the sitters' vanities. What one writer describes as 'insipid idealism' became fashionable and at the beginning of the 18th century prettiness and superficial charm were the qualities sought for by miniaturists. Miniatures in enamel first became the vogue in George I's reign, an art most practised by foreign artists working in England and the artist Richard Cosway appeared on an artistic wave that carried such men as Gainsborough, Reynolds, Hogarth and Romney to fame, and our miniature painting had a magnificent revival. Artists of this period were outstanding in all fields. Nollekens, the sculptor, Zoffany, Bartolozzi and Angelica Kauffman added their genious to the tide of creative art.

Richard Cosway was probably the master of the miniaturists of this period but there were a host of other excellent artists in the same field. Jeremiah Meyer, for instance, was appointed enamel

A charming miniature of Mary Louisa Inglis by George Engleheart. She wears a white lace bonnet and a low-cut frock. Her name and 'aged 6 years 1795' are inscribed on the frame which has woven hair inset at the back.

(Courtesy of Sotheby & Co.)

painter to George III and miniature painter to the Queen, whilst Nathaniel Hone was an oil-painter who turned to water-colours and then enamels; and Richard Collins (1755–1831) a pupil of Jeremiah Meyer, was also a miniature and enamel painter to George III.

Richard Cosway's famous miniature of the right eye of Mrs. Fitzherbert, made as a present for her to give to the Prince Regent, may well have started the fashion, lasting into Victorian days, when these love-tokens of eyes were mounted in rings or bracelets and brooches and even in snuff-boxes. Another miniaturist who produced eye portraits was George Engleheart, who was one of Sir Joshua Reynolds' pupils and he exhibited at the Royal Academy between 1773 and 1812. Cosway's style was specially suited to work on ivory, a brilliant and transparent surface that needed swift and sensitive painting of unerring accuracy. The charm and delicacy of his style is brilliant and individual and does not easily lend itself to being copied, which is just as well for the collector, as he has to be prepared for innumerable copyists' work and to be able to distinguish the master artist from the copyist by inferior technique and also by the lack of a signature. When you consider that George Engleheart painted no less than 4,853 miniatures in the course of less than forty years, and then think of the large number of other miniaturists working at the same period, and their copyists, the collector has to know his homework very well indeed to choose the master from the pupil or the copyist.

We have now come full circle back to John Smart with whom we began this short study and he was in fact one of the few artists in this field who earned Richard Cosway's praise and for a time at least was his friend. His 'surprising likenesses' was his special asset as well as a finish to his portraits so smooth that it looks almost like enamel. He usually signed J.S., as we have seen, and the Victoria and Albert Museum and the Wallace Collection have fine examples of his work, as well as of other famous miniaturists.

One word of warning; there are many forgeries masquerading as genuine miniatures and it is as well to study your subject well before embarking on a costly purchase. One clue, besides the poor technique and bad drawing, is that the ivories are usually polished on both sides. The best policy is to spend a long time studying this beautiful art in museums and with reputable dealers.

The signatures of the master miniature painters are usually found as either monograms or initials on the portraits themselves, when a very strong magnifying glass will be required to discover them; or else a full signature may be on the back of the ivory or vellum. Certain artists, including Samuel Cooper and Richard Cosway, made use of monograms but the majority used small initials, like Flatman's F. and T.F. and Isaac Oliver's I.O. and Nicholas Hilliard's N.H. Thomas Flatman also used a monogram, and George Engleheart used both E. and G.E.

II

Our miniature painters are represented on snuff-boxes and Horace Walpole's collection included 'a fine gold escalop snuff-box' which was mounted in the 18th century with miniatures by Hilliard of James I and of Queen Elizabeth, which of course they had never been intended to decorate. Miniaturists copied portraits by masters as we know, but presumably Walpole's were original and simply mounted on the gold box later. Miniatures appeared on boxes in England from about 1720. The French had been making gold snuff-boxes since about 1660 but *boîtes-à-portrait* are not recorded until 1668. However these were not preserved, as the recipients changed the boxes into hard cash and only kept

A large circular Games Box by Raven (unsigned) the lid painted with *Dignity and Impudence* after Landseer.

(*Courtesy of Sotheby & Co.*)

the miniature portraits. Our own goldsmiths were influenced by the French and decorations in enamel with flowers and classical patterns in French style appear on our gold boxes of the 1760–80 period. Richard Cosway and others painted miniatures for these boxes. Henry Bone (1755–1834) copied a portrait of George IV in 1823 from Lawrence's picture of him as Prince Regent for a gold box.

Less expensively another miniature of George IV after Lawrence, painted by Samuel Raven, appears on a papier-mâché snuff-box circa 1825, which is in the Victoria and Albert Museum. Samuel Raven (1775–1847) was a painter who is generally associated with papier-mâché boxes produced at Birmingham and he usually signed his name inside the lid, though alas his boxes are generally damaged and are few and far between. The German family called Stobwasser were making similar boxes at the same time, painting copies of pictures by French, Dutch, Spanish, Italian and English artists on the lids. These are also usually signed and there are

Portrait inscribed Mlle. H. Sonntag on a Stobwasser papier-mâché snuff-box. Georg Siegmund Stobwasser was granted exclusive rights in 1769 in Brunswick to produce japanned furniture, trays, snuff-boxes etc., continuing well into the 19th century.

(Courtesy of Sotheby & Co.)

George IV painted *after Lawrence* on a Stobwasser box inscribed inside 'Stobwasser's Fabrik'.

(Courtesy of Sotheby & Co.)

many of these about. The French boxes of papier-mâché were varnished with *vernis Martin* named after Robert Martin who invented it. They used portraits of famous people like Napoleon, Marie-Louise and others to decorate their lids.

Miniature landscapes and figures, even portraits of animals, are delightful additions to French and English and German snuff-boxes made out of ivory, tortoiseshell, lacquered wood and papier-mâché. Those exquisite English enamelled boxes, which have scenes and portraits on them, were often painted by the enamellists from French *scènes galantes* by Boucher, Lancret, Watteau and others. These were made both in Staffordshire and at Battersea and English artists like Charles Fenn and Robert Hancock also figure on them.

A visit to such French museums as the *Musée des Arts Décoratifs*, the *Louvre* and the *Musée Cognacq-Jay* will delight collectors who are interested in miniature painting on small French boxes of all kinds. They excelled in this delicate art.

III

Wax Portraits

One of the most exciting moments for a collector is the unexpected discovery of a long sought-after treasure in a totally unforeseen place. I count myself fortunate to have had such an experience.

I was prowling round in search of small silver and, after a pleasant talk with a dealer friend, prepared for departure. Happening to turn and glance up at a picture above a display cabinet, there in a bird's eye maplewood frame I saw a collection of no fewer than seven wax portraits, all modelled before 1820. An inscription, in spidery copperplate on the back of the frame, read:

May. 1820

Within this and the 23 other frames which are its fellows I have placed my Collection of Waxen Portraiture :- Likenesses of those Famous and Infamous, living and long since Dead, which I have gathered during my Peregrinations up and down and round about the World.   J. St. E.

Very little has been written about waxes but one of the best collections is fortunately in our Wallace Collection in Manchester Square, London. There you will find, Italian, German and French wax portraits to demonstrate the finest examples of the medium;

amongst them is the famous diptych of the Duc de Guise and his wife, which is one of the earliest known coloured portraits of this kind.

Some of the loveliest waxes are Italian; after flourishing in the 15th century they reached their peak in the 16th, when tiny jewels and silk, velvet and even hair were used to add reality to the portraits. The Italian Renaissance was the highest point in the achievement of the artist in wax, and most of the early examples are works of art in their own right, unconnected with medals. Usually they are mounted on ovals, sometimes as little as two inches in height, though sometimes as much as twelve inches. Backgrounds were of wax or blue or brown glass, though by the 1780's they were often mounted on black or crimson velvet. By the nineteenth century you will find pale Regency-green backgrounds. Usually the glass in the frames is convex and the frames are of gilt, rosewood, pearwood and black turned-wood in the 18th century. Satinwood and maplewood were used as well in the 19th.

Such a fragile material is unfortunately subject to the ravages of time, so that the very earliest of all waxes are difficult to trace. It is one of the oldest of the arts and we can be sure that modelling in beeswax was practised as early as 400 B.C. The ancient Egyptians modelled wax fruits and small figures to put in the tombs beside their illustrious dead in order to refresh and keep them company on their last journey.

Michelangelo worked in wax and a portrait of him, attributed to Leone Leoni, one of the best artists of his period, is now in the British Museum. Quite early artists experimented in formulas of wax; plain beeswax was found to be unsuitable since it became badly discoloured with age. The tools used originally were probably much the same as those of bone, ivory and wood that artists used in the 18th century, though most of the modelling was always done with thumb and fingers.

Modelling in wax was used by the early sculptors, goldsmiths and artists in bronze as a means to their ends. The medallists, for instance, always modelled their portraits in wax before taking plaster or sulphur casts from them for medallions in bronze or other metals. The sculptors too would often make a small wax figure of a proposed work. The wax modeller at his best in fact had to combine the skills of the miniature painter, the sculptor and the goldsmith; though probably it is the medallist who is his nearest parallel. It is the portrait in wax which is an end in itself that is the work of art prized by collectors.

In England the early history is obscure, but we do know that Antoine Benoist, who modelled coloured wax at the court of Louis XIV, came to England on a short visit in 1684 to make portraits of James II and his courtiers. He may indeed have been responsible for introducing coloured wax modelling to England for, although wax effigies had been used at the state funerals of our kings from the 13th century, it is not until early in the 18th that wax portraiture was adopted by English artists.

Its heyday in England, when wax portraiture was most popular, began in the middle of the 18th century and lasted until roughly 1840. After that the art declined, although Richard Cockle Lucas, who died in 1883, made excellent medallion portraits of many famous Victorians.

Gainsborough used to make miniatures of his friends from candle-ends. One of his first efforts however was the ass's head he showed to the sculptor Nollekens for his expert advice. 'You should model more with your thumbs,' advised Nollekens. 'Thumb it about till you get it into shape.'

Artists used plain white, red or yellow coloured wax. The composition was generally beeswax mixed with lard, flour and diachylon, a kind of sticky plaster. This formula did not differ much from from that used in the 16th century.

Perhaps the most oustanding wax miniaturist of the 18th century was Samuel Percy, who died in 1820. An Irishman, born in 1750, his portraits are very remarkable and much admired by the connoisseur. He modelled in high relief in pink or white wax, and the details of wigs, clothing and features were particularly delicately modelled and skilfully coloured. He also produced amusing scenes of country life, and another of his specialities was 'dead wax likenesses done bracelet size after the manner of Roman coins'.

Another name to remember is that of Isaac Gosset. He came from a Huguenot family that took refuge in Jersey. In passing it is amusing to learn that one of his family earned a precarious living there from knitting garments which he christened 'Jerseys'. Isaac

Gosset made brilliant lifelike profiles of the royal family which were in great demand. The wax he used, a lovely ivory colour, was his speciality, but unfortunately he seldom seems to have signed his work. As a rule he used blue glass or a wine-coloured background for his portraits.

James Tassie is another important name of the 18th century; he is represented in the Scottish National Portrait Gallery by more than 150 of his forceful coloured portraits. He used a good deal of pink wax mounted on thick Bristol blue glass grounds.

Patience Wright, a Quaker working between 1772 and 1786, was an American who came to England at the age of 47, an old lady by the standards of her day, and joined the number of women modellers in wax. She became a great friend of the King and Queen and, from an early start as a child who made bread and candle-ends into likenesses of her friends, she developed into a successful artist in her middle age.

There are many other names which the collector will discover in the pursuit of his quarry. It is worth adding the name of Catharine Andras, perhaps, to the present necessarily arbitrary list. She was born in Bristol in 1775 and continued her fashionable business until 1824. One of her famous models was Lord Nelson, who is reported to have said to her that he was not used to 'being taken in that manner, starboard and larboard at the same time'. She went on working with the same skill to the ripe old age of eighty.

Collectors sometimes complain that very few waxes are signed; though this is true to a certain extent, nevertheless you may enjoy all the excitement of the chase by searching carefully with a strong magnifying glass in unexpected places. First of all look at the usual place, which was the cut-away part below the shoulders of the bust portraits. Then try the wax ground; or sometimes the signature is scratched on the glass ground or into the paint or it may be painted on a wood ground in an obscure corner.

Yes, there were fakes, particularly of the early Renaissance period. Waxes are unfortunately comparatively easy to forge. But we may take comfort from the fact that the lack of demand for 18th century waxes has made it unprofitable for the faker to try his hand very much on this delicate art—as yet. The best way to defeat him is to go and look at the authentic examples in the Victoria and Albert Museum, the Wallace Collection, the National

Portrait Galleries in London and Edinburgh and, if you are in Paris, go to the Louvre, the Musée Carnavalet and the Musée de Cluny.

The historic interest of waxes, as well as their beauty and romantic charm, makes the search for these delicate, fragile miniatures a most rewarding pursuit.

16th century wax portraits of Claude de Loraine, Duc de Guise, and his wife, Antoinette de Bourbon, in contemporary hinged leather-case. Claude was the grandfather of Mary, Queen of Scots.

(Courtesy of The Wallace Collection)

MINIATURE POTTERY AND PORCELAIN

I

Toy China

The most obvious miniatures in the field of ceramics are the baby house wares, the tiny objects for kitchen and dining-room and for ornamenting shelves or cabinets. These were being made on the Continent by European potters from the 16th century: and in Nüremberg dinner-sets and kitchen ware with designs of flowers, birds and fruit were being hand-painted in brilliant colours on green or white ground very early on, about 1550.

Even such famous potters as Philip Elers, who was responsible for bringing saltglaze technique to England from his native Holland, is believed to have made some for baby houses. There is a diminutive tea-set of saltglaze, which has raised figures on it, and this is no further away than our own British Museum. The London Museum too boasts a good collection of miniature china and a number of mouth-watering dishes of dolls' house food as well, dating to about 1850, with the food on the plates modelled out of plaster and brightly painted in appropriate colours.

A charming dolls' dinner service from Staffordshire is in this Museum decorated in blue transfer on a white ground, showing a village green, on which children are playing with a kite and a hoop. An old man looks at the large milestone and behind the figures are trees, a church and a mansion. The service is late 19th century with a much earlier transfer design, the figures being dressed in early 19th century clothes. Presumably the potters used the same patterns for many consecutive years.

Miniature cream ware can be found and Whieldon tea-sets, as well as Leeds sets for dinner with feather edges to the plates or tea sets from this factory with even the refinement of pierced decoration. Swansea, Spode, Worcester, Coalport and Davenport all produced dolls' or children's tea and dinner-sets. Probably

Doll's dinner service. Staffordshire blue-and-white
china. Late 19th century. Diameter of plate is $3\frac{1}{2}$ inches.
(*Courtesy of the London Museum*)

some of these beautifully made small pieces were originally intended as samples to be carried by the traveller to solicit orders. The tiny little teapots are very enchanting and rarities like a pap-boat occasionally appear to delight collectors. Besides the elegant porcelain pieces there were countless sets in the 19th century made out of expendable heavy china, cheerfully decorated with flowers and gold borders. Although many miniature toy pieces are not marked, better class wares do turn up with makers' marks on them. A dinner service in printed earthenware, comprising all the necessities an adult sized set would have required, is a rare find if complete. The porcelain examples would find their way to the great salerooms as they are expensive, rare and beautifully made.

It is as well to bear in mind the fact that tablewares in these small sizes are being made today in France, Germany, Japan, England and elsewhere too, I daresay. Tourist shops in Paris sell miniature tea-sets, candlesticks, chairs and tables and pianos, dog-kennels and other trivia in porcelain, but these are not meant to deceive antique collectors, of course.

Children's as distinct from dolls' tableware is small too and there are some very attractive children's plates and mugs, usually with transfer prints of nursery rhymes or improving verses, sports, alphabets and other educational subjects and biblical themes; some from Swansea with gaily coloured embossed flowers on the rims and some with such sentiments as 'A Present for Robert' or 'A Present for a good Girl' inscribed on them. These charming plates and mugs were chiefly found, no doubt, at fairgrounds and they were obviously much appreciated for so many to have survived the wear and tear or nursery life. Few of them are marked, but I have seen 'W.S. & Co' on some, which were made by William Smith and Co., a firm from Stockton-on-Tees which also exported them abroad[1]: The Paris 'flea-markets' sometimes produce these and a more sophisticated version for adults with Punch-like jokes about crinolines or railways, for example. Baily and Ball of Longton made attractive octagonal shapes plates with embossed borders and circular red or green or blue lines dividing the patterns. Inside many different pictures of Robinson Crusoe and other nursery subjects were printed and the border design was first registered in March 1847.

[1] *Antique China and Glass under £5* by Geoffrey A. Godden, F.R.S.A.

Akin to these children's gift plates are the amusing little plates about 3 inches wide with views printed on them of the seaside. These were made both at Swansea and Sunderland. They were meant for the eating of cockles. Some are a bit larger and have designs of fish and shells on them.

The pottery money-boxes for children are crudely made, as they were obviously expendable. The only way to extract the child's savings was the clumsy effort with a knife in the slit for the coin, which often damaged the slit if it did not destroy the whole 'piggy-bank'. Lions, cocks, beehives, dogs, chests of drawers, cottages, bottles, fishes; the catalogue of different models is long.

II
Mostly Ornaments

Toys or images, as they were called, unmarked and mostly made in the potteries of Staffordshire, were produced in several sizes and innumerable patterns from about 1840 to 1900. They were later re-issued, so that the untutored collector is nowadays under-

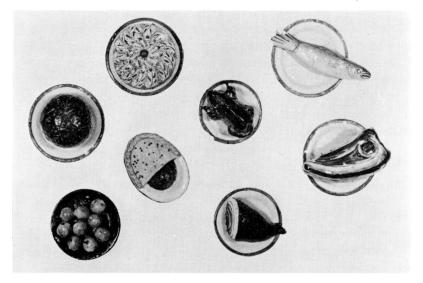

Doll's food. Plaster painted in bright colours. The dishes represent a traditional meal of Christmas pudding, roast chicken, baked ham, a half-eaten black-currant pie, a dish of apples, a cream cake, a trout and a rib of beef. *c.* 1850. The plates are $1\frac{3}{4}$ inches in diameter.

(Courtesy of the London Museum)

A pair of 'image toys' made in Staffordshire *c.* 1850. They represent the Prince of Wales and the Princess Royal on horseback.

Staffordshire pottery cradle of Napoleon's unfortunate son *Le Roi de Rome*, who was born in 1811. The colours are soft yellow and strong royal blue round the edges.

standably chary about buying them. There are many specialist dealers to whom he may turn, however, for help and advice and a number of reference books too. These figures are so gay and lively that they bring great vitality to a nursery or a kitchen, if they are not placed cheek by jowl with the best Derby cat or Chelsea shepherdess. Compared with the 18th century potters of course they are neither so well-potted nor do they have the individual character of their ancestors. For one thing they are mostly moulded in two pieces, the decoration being applied by home-based painters and very often by children; for another, they were the product of an industrial age, already beginning to believe in mass-production rather than the handmade articles. The Royal Family, prominent politicians, generals and patriotic figures were popular, and a complete history of the period could be collected, including religious, poetic, sporting, acting, socially-minded figures, not to mention murderers and their victims. There are still many figures that have not been identified and collectors avidly search through contemporary magazines and newspapers, prints and music sheets for lithographs or engravings that were used as models for the figures. The fame of some of them is lasting, whilst the stories of others are lost.

It looks as if the most profitable collection would be one of named figures, and those made between Queen Victoria's accession and about 1850. These figures are good colours, with that pleasant ultramarine blue and sprigs of flowers and coloured wavy lines on the dresses and waistcoats. They are true peasant art and have no pretensions to niceties of modelling or even to strict portraiture. The book that at this time of writing which is still the best basic book on the subject is *Staffordshire Portrait Figures of the Victorian Age* by Thomas Balston.

Although we tend to think of these 'toys' or chimney ornaments as Staffordshire, they were also being made by North Country and Scottish potteries like Portobello, Bo'ness and Watson's Pottery at Prestonpans. The ornaments known as 'dabbities' in Scotland are akin to the Staffordshire Prattware. They come from Portobello and their unmistakable palette is underglaze blue, green, yellow and a sort of purple-brown, which is sometimes dabbed on by a brush or sponged on and sometimes painted with spots. Bo'ness Pottery in Linlithgow employed potters, painters

A collection of 19th century German China fairings intended for the English bazaar trade. These are highly coloured and mostly trinket or pin-boxes. The 3 oblong boxes in the bottom row are matchboxes, having serrated edges for striking phosphorus matches.

Model of a booth at a fair. Staffordshire, about 1830. Height: $13\frac{1}{4}$ inches. (*Courtesy of the Fitzwilliam Museum, Cambridge*)

and printers from Staffordshire, and from about 1836 until it closéd in 1889[1]. Bo'ness is a contraction of Borrowstounness. They specialized in chimney ornaments, especially pairs of birds and animals. Dogs standing on four feet and without pedestals were the ones known as 'comforters', as well as fox-terriers and other breeds, cats and rabbits.

The field of Scottish pottery has been much neglected. One reason may have been that only *one* Scottish factory, the Glasgow Pottery, which was started early in the 19th century by John and Matthew Perston Bell, exhibited at the Great Exhibition of 1851. Yet there were at least eighty reasonably large potteries in production then, as well as many small family concerns.

What is loosely called peasant pottery, or sometimes popular or folk art, is another neglected field. Here we have to distinguish from the true makers of rather crude, gaily coloured pottery found abroad in places like Alsace, Brittany and the Netherlands and the imitations produced by sophisticated modern potters, who are not at all naïve. The interesting part about these simple wares is that they have a common denominator which shows a distinct family kinship, regardless of the country of origin. The French cockerels and flowers on the faience dishes have the same kind of charming bold, colourful, vigorous patterns that enliven our Staffordshire, Scottish and Welsh and other pottery.

Village potters often made their wares as a side line to their everyday work as, for example, farmers. They supplied local people with crocks needed for everyday use and also for special occasions like holidays and festivals, weddings, christenings or any great events that might take place. The miniature cradles decorated with slipware come under this category. They were given as commemoration gifts to friends. Loving cups, posset pots, plates in many sizes, picture plaques to hang on the walls,

[1]*English and Scottish Earthenware* by G. Bernard Hughes. 'Bo'ness Potteries (Linlithgow) were established in 1766 as The South Pottery.' Acquired by Dr. John Roebuck in 1784, it 'operated under a succession of managements in the 19th century.' Mr. Geoffrey Godden found a child's mug marked 'Industrial Pottery, Bo'ness' and traced its origin to the 'Industrial Co-operative Pottery Society' of Grange Pans, Bo'ness, which apparently closed in 1894, the parent concern having been registered in 1887. Over now to anyone interested in sorting out this little problem of dates and factories.

and the harvest jugs, big and small, made in Wales, Devon, Somerset, Kent and elsewhere in the 17th and 18th centuries. Staffordshire was always the most prolific in output of the potters' craft. The harvest pottery, in particular that coming from North Devon, has a striking similarity to Continental styles of the same type. Examples of these pots can be seen at the Taunton Museum: for example there is a smallish earthenware dish, dated 1680, with a scratched design on it commemorating the birth of Siamese twins. This celebrated birth also appeared on a delft charger about the same time.[1] The Toft family, whose name appears written on so many slip decorated earthenware plates and dishes of the 17th century is probably the best known of these named and dated wares, and museums like the Victoria and Albert Museum and the Hanley Museum at Stoke-on-Trent have examples. But here we are digressing, as these earthenware pieces were not, so far as I know, made in small sizes.

There were enchanting miniature Bristol made earthenware barrels, painted with flowers and other decorations. A pair of red earthenware lions incised 'H. Davies, Pill Pottery' of the early 19th century are in the Fitzwilliam Museum, Cambridge, looking very quaint and folk-art-like.

St. Peter's Pottery at Newcastle-on-Tyne was established by Thomas Fell and the early pieces, notably a smug-looking lamb, which is at the Victoria and Albert Museum, certainly qualify this factory for a place amongst our peasant pottery class.

III
Candle-Snuffers

A few years ago a friend came to lunch and brought with her the wholly unexpected and entirely delightful gift of a diminutive dolls' house size Derby chamber candlestick, marked on the base unmistakably.[2] This little porcelain gem has graced the best bedroom of a castellated mid-Victorian dolls' house ever since. The only thing it obviously never had and I have never seen a lilliputian one, was a candle-snuffer.

[1] See *English Delftware* by F. H. Garner.

[2] The Derby factory closed in 1848—The Royal Crown Derby factory started production in the 1870's.

Scissor-snuffers date back to the birth of candles, as the early ones required constant care and trimming of the wicks, and these were of course made of metal. They usually occupied a silver, pewter or brass tray and the snuffers, like the trays, were fitted with little feet to stand upon. In Victorian days 'douters' or extinguishers, shaped like a dunce's cap, were used and trays in the early 19th century carried a pair of these. Of course those cone-shaped snuffers on the end of a long handle have a much longer lineage, dating to medieval days, when they were used, and for that matter still are used, for putting out the tall candles in churches. They used to be in demand for putting out the candles on chandeliers, which can have been no light job in every sense of the word.

Victorian servants were often told to remove candles from the dinner-table in order to snuff them, as it was all too easy to let the wax fall on the polished table or even on the food. The amusing snuffers that we are here most concerned with are the charming and diverse examples, all variations of the dunce's cap shape, which were many of them made at the Worcester factory, probably few dating earlier than 1870. Some are marked, and there are a great assortment of porcelain figures of this 1870-90 period as well. The Chinese lady, modelled by James Hadley and shown at the Vienna Exhibition of 1873, bears a strong family resemblance to a Chinese lady squatting on her haunches eating rice from a yellow bowl. She wears a green kimono, dusted with white flowers and a vermilion pair of trousers and a yellow sash. She is a candle-snuffer. A more appropriate figure is that of a man in his voluminous white dressing gown with green sprigs on it and wearing a red nightcap. He is modelled in earthenware. Another Worcester snuffer is shaped like a stout old lady in an apron and cap with very rosy cheeks, and the most elegant of this small collection is a girl in a regional head-dress with a 'jewelled' motif on her cap and collar, similar to the special service made for the Countess of Derby in 1865.[1] This tea service has women's heads painted, inside ovals, by Thomas Callowhill, the jewelling as well as the gilding having been carried out by Samuel Randford. The heads certainly

[1] See p. 379 in Godden's *Illustrated Encyclopaedia of British Pottery and Porcelain.*

resemble the candle-snuffer, but there is no identifying mark.

There are also ceramic candle-snuffers in the shape of owls and hats, and very collectable they are, in their rather childish way. They will never be made again now that chamber candlesticks have passed into history.

IV

Cow-Creamers

Looking round a collectors cabinet recently I was amazed at what a number of animals there were represented in miniature sizes. They appeared in silver, brass, ormolu, pottery, porcelain and glass. There were cats and dogs, elephants, giraffes, zebras and horses, birds of many kinds and cows. These last were standing together in a herd and perhaps these cow-creamers might serve as an illustration of the group by virtue of their originality. The purist may quibble and ask if anyone has ever seen a miniature cow-creamer. Not I, alas, though I have a cow butter dish in two-inch size as well as hen tureens the same tiny dimensions, both in glass and in pottery. Nevertheless the cow-creamers are miniature cows; and if any other excuse is needed, these ludicrous but endearing creatures have appealed to me for so many years, surely others share my delight in them.

Tea, tay or tcha is mentioned favourably by Pepys, but the real addict was Dr. Johnson, who admitted that he was 'a hardened and shameless tea-drinker', sipping it at all hours and confessing that he welcomed the morning with it, amused the evening with it and finally solaced midnight with it. In Paris, on the other hand, the tea was not at all to his liking, particularly when his hostess, finding the teapot would not pour satisfactorily, ordered the footman to blow into the spout.

Milk was supplied with the tea, though there is some controversy as to whether it was served hot or cold at first. Most likely it was heated and brought to the table in a tall jug to match the teapot, just the same as that which accompanied the coffee pot.

Somewhere about 1750 the Dutch silversmith David Willaume the Younger produced a witty addition to the tea table in the shape of a milk jug modelled as a cow. Actually, John Schuppe is the name we particularly associate with these silver cow-creamers. He entered his mark at Goldsmiths Hall in 1753 and specialized in them. An example dated 1755 is in the Victoria and Albert Museum in company with five other specimens. However, there appears to be conclusive evidence from hall-marks that David Willaume the Younger made them before Schuppe. But experts are cautious about who invented the idea.

These silver Georgian cows are now prodigiously expensive. Sometimes they were gilded and a crest might be engraved on the body. They were made in sections, and occasionally wore inscribed collars or had a bell hanging round their necks. The saddle was always mounted by a fly and it opened up to allow the milk to fill the cow's hollow body. Holding the cow by the tail, the lady of the house could pour milk from the cow's open mouth.

This ingenious joke had already caught on with the potters. The Hanley Museum, Stoke-on-Trent, has a magnificent collection of more than 700 of these entertaining creatures. The earliest is a Delft pottery example made about 1720. It also has a Stoke-on-Trent salt-glazed creamer which is no later than 1740, as well as several lead-glazed cows belonging to the 1740–60 period.

Our potters produced a delightfully varied herd, which, to judge by the numbers, must have been very much to the taste of the 18th and 19th century tea drinkers. Thomas Whieldon is always said to have been the first English potter to produce cow milk jugs, but in fact the earliest lead-glazed cows cannot be definitely attributed to him; though, for that matter, nor is there any proof that he did not invent them. Certainly he made salt-glazed ware, but the specialists prefer to call these cow-creamers 'Whieldon type'. In any case they remained fashionable for nearly a century, and by 1815 they had become popular enough to be sold at the fairs for a few pence.

The 18th century cows are the most desirable. These early ones had rectangular openings in their backs, but by the end of the century the holes were round. Look for the authentic unglazed lower rims of the plinths on which the cows stand. They were made in white and brown salt-glazed ware, pearl ware and dark red earthenware, as well as Staffordshire bone china. Derby made examples in soft-paste porcelain.

Like the silver jugs, these cows were made in several parts and the body was cast in two halves. The ones produced before 1830 look rough inside. You will find dappled-tan, black and grey, yellow, blue and pink cows. Sometimes the horns and hoofs are painted in a contrasting green or yellow.

The Pratts of Fenton and the Sunderland potters were prolific makers of cow-creamers. Dixon Phillips and Co. made them and theirs are sometimes marked and can therefore be dated between 1840 and 1865. Some of these, as well as the early ones, have no curly tails to serve as handles. It has been suggested that these were in fact pastille burners but, while the picture of a pottery cow breathing out scented smoke from its lowing mouth is an appealing one, it sounds highly improbable.

The Glamorgan pottery works at Swansea made a great number of cow-creamers, and they were noted especially for decorating them with transfer printing. Leeds made examples of these cows, and so did Rockingham, Tyneside, Portobello and Prestonpans.

In Staffordshire lustre ware was frequently used; the old lustre with its bubbly, irregular spots appears golden in a strong light, which modern reproductions never do. There are charming cow-creamers sponged with black and ochre, standing on a green base and sometimes accompanied by milkmaids. The cows often have kicking-straps round their back legs.

Balfour's North British pottery issued a successful series of cow-creamers about 1874, the cow standing on a green oval plinth. These late ones must have been made more for decoration than use, for the 19th century became more concerned with hygiene after the outbreak of cholera which spread into Europe from Asia. Lady Louisa Molyneux wrote to the diarist Creevy in 1833, 'Reeves cannot get people to drink his French wine, entirely from fear of cholera'. The London outbreak in 1848 gave the final clue to Dr. John Snow, who discovered that cholera was contracted from contaminated drinking water. The cow creamers, so impossible to clean properly, naturally lost favour, though both the silver-smiths and the potters made them until the end of the century.

A fine English silver cow-creamer dated 1865, by Richard Hennell, a member of the famous family of silversmiths, is one of the later ones which are nevertheless desirable, owing to the excellence of the work. They cost much less than their Georgian relations but more than the Dutch and German ones of the 19th century. A herd of these cows, with import marks before 1900, say, are not to be despised, since fine silver maintains its value.

They were still being exported in 1920, but are most of them Victorian, with a delightful, naïve charm, not unlike the humorous pottery ones.

A herd of pottery cows would cost you less, and if it is colour you are seeking and that particular, vigorous, lively freshness which is the speciality of our native potters, then you could do no better than search for pottery cow-creamers, keeping as usual a wary eyes open for reproductions. Pottery reproductions, of course, have no intrinsic value as do the cow creamers made of silver. A collection of the pottery cows would illustrate over a hundred years of the changes in English pottery both in technique and in decoration.

One last word: look out for that rare and paradoxical creature the bull creamer! One collector spent nearly a life-time before he found one. The potter who invented him must have caused some hilarious laughter. Possibly he even inspired Dr. Johnson with one of his bons mots. 'Truth, sir,' he said to the ever attentive Boswell, 'is a cow which will yield sceptics no more milk, and so they are gone to milk the bull.' Recently a friend told me he had seen a goat-creamer; this must be another rarity, or perhaps only a curiosity.

RINGS

I

A little History and other matters

This book, as will readily be seen, is no great work contributing to scholarship distilled from a lifetime of research. It does not break new ground but is intended to stimulate interest and encourage the collector by drawing attention to the wide scope available to him even in small and sometimes forgotten antiques. For the specialist there are excellent books available in public libraries and museums, and these have been written by scholarly experts who have devoted their time to the research in depth of one particular subject.

Meanwhile, scratching on the surface with undiminished enthusiasm, the rewards for the amateur, in its original meaning, are countless. Ferreting about in market-stalls has more than once resulted in unusual finds and the detective instinct, dominant in most collectors, is aroused so that off he goes to books, museums and knowledgeable friends in order to identify his latest discovery.

Side by side with the irresistible search for a bargain goes the more sensible and ultimately far more rewarding purchase from the best dealer that we can find in our own particular quarry of the moment. Jewellery is a case in point, as so often skimmed milk masquerades as cream in this field. Gigi's[1] first lesson in fine stones as a schoolgirl came from her Aunt Alicia, when she mistakenly called a yellow diamond a topaz, to the old courtesan's great indignation. Gigi was instructed on the only jewellery advisable to accept from admirers. Although rubies, sapphires and emeralds would do, provided they were of the best quality, the only really sensible stones to ask for were the largest possible diamonds and the most expensive pearls to be found. For some

[1] *Gigi* by Colette.

133

reason Aunt Alicia was dead against 'artistic jewellery' and all those attractive pieces we admire so much today like cameos, lyres, stars and so forth. These Gigi was to avoid; which all goes to show how much fashion dictates our taste.

Whether men will ever go back to wearing enormous rings and expensive jewels sewn on to their clothes, hung round their necks or in their ears is debatable; but women will surely never forego these ornaments. Primitive societies, now so nostalgically copied by Western man in their dance and music, wear jewellery a great deal, carrying their wealth round the necks of warriors and wives alike; the only difference being that the men wear the larger and finer jewels for reasons of prestige, as well as for magic protection.

In Tudor days the ostentatious courtier would not only be covered with jewels all over his clothes and tricked out in earrings and bejewelled shoes, but his many-ringed fingers often toyed with a loose precious stone to show off his riches. Those lovely mermaids designed from an irregular pearl, or the emerald dolphin are from this period's inspiration. In Elizabeth I's days the Emperor Charles V possessed an earring incorporating a tiny little chiming watch. As for Louis XIV's gem-conscious court, his was one of the most extravagantly glittering palaces in Europe. The Sun King was born in 1638 and his long reign lasted from 1643 to 1715, whilst in England Charles I was ruling, followed by Oliver Cromwell, Charles II, James II, William and Mary, Queen Anne and the first year of George I's reign.

Inevitably during our Civil War family silver and family jewellery was melted down or sold to bring in funds to enable the Royalists to pay their soldiers; but although the Puritans reacted violently against jewellery, they approved, perhaps not surprisingly, those macabre reminders of the brevity of life, jewels in the form of death's-heads or coffins with skeletons inside made out of precious stones, silver or gold; and they also permitted 'mortality jewellery' like mourning rings woven from the hair of the dear departed. These mementoes continued to be popular, especially in middle-class families, for the next two hundred years.

Mourning rings are often collected and the romantic themes of the 1830's with urns and weeping willows and mourning ladies beside them give a melancholy grace to the fashion for contemplating death and decay, or dwelling on unrequited love and any other hopeless cause. Jet was useful in this group and the French made use of black glass which was called 'French jet'. Black enamel rings set with pearl and diamond flowers and encircled with engraved gold are particularly attractive pieces of mourning jewellery of the 19th century.

This century saw the decline of craftsmanship in jewellery, for the average man began to think more of amassing money than amassing jewellery and the stern example of Beau Brummell decreed that men at least should scorn glitter, romance and colour, putting the diamonds showily on their wives heads, necks or hands and themselves wearing nothing more impressive than a signet ring and perhaps a very small scarf-pin. Poor Disraeli in his flamboyant way shocked London Society by wearing his magnificent diamond-set rings over his gloves when he first took his seat in Parliament. This was in 1837 and not only was nobody amused, but Disraeli did not set a fashion, as he may have hoped, but merely caused considerable indignation.

The only way modern man can enjoy jewellery is to collect it, and even then his wife is afraid to wear it lest thieves take note and decide to steal it. The more enterprising might care to set their wits to work on trying to salvage that incredibly richly bound copy of the Omar Khayyam sent to an American purchaser in the ill-fated Titanic in 1912. It was said to have had well over a thousand jewels incorporated into an exciting design of peacocks and poppies, grapes and deadly nightshade in the Art Nouveau style of the period. But probably it is beyond redemption now.

Memorial rings, as we have seen, are not confined to the 19th century and bequesting them by will to worthy recipients dates back to very early days. A certain Bishop of Chichester, for instance, bequeathed two rings to Henry III, one set with an emerald and the other with a ruby, both stones having magical properties. Anne of Cleves, fortunate enough to have survived Henry VIII, left several mourning rings to various friends and even Shakespeare willed money to his friends for buying themselves rings in his memory.

However, it is the 18th and early 19th century ones we are most likely to find and very decorative and handsome they are, these miniature pictures in their gold rimmed setting, sometimes enamelled, sometimes studded with pearls and often inscribed with a name and date. Others have portrait miniatures without the little landscape of urn and willow which is the classical type.

The skulls and skeletons engraved on rings were not in memoriam but as a reminder of life's brevity. Luther apparently had a gold one with a little enamelled death's-head in its centre. Sometimes the portraits were not displayed but hidden behind a precious or semi-precious stone setting and often the deceased persons' hair was plaited into the design. There were also 'reliquary' or 'pilgrim' rings. The British Museum has one called the Coventry ring, made of gold. It is of 15th century origin. These rings were either carved with some religious words or else they had some little relic inside them of a saint or perhaps a chip purporting to come from the Cross.

Wedding rings have altered little in the years between the 20th century and the Saxon days, when they were recorded as traditional practice in use at weddings. Christians were using marriage rings in 860, and the Romans had betrothal rings and after the marriage settlement was signed rings were distributed, engraved with the newly wedded couples' names, to the assembled guests. Only about 150 years ago the Prince Regent handed round a number of rings to friends and relatives on his marriage to poor Queen Caroline and Queen Victoria also distributed gold rings on her marriage to Prince Albert. These had her profile on them. I wonder if any of them are still around today.

II

Collectable Rings

The 19th century, as we have seen, is probably the best hunting-ground for collectors, since earlier rings are comparatively rare. Besides the mourning rings there are beautiful designs in souvenir rings made from such unexpected materials as Blue John fluospar, shell cameos, lava and mosaic. These date from about 1837. This, the date of Queen Victoria's accession, is also roughly the date we associate with clusters of gems that are set into rather narrow bands, and the flowers are made of enamel and gems, particularly the romantic forget-me-nots and pansies. Those rather forbidding serpents, with glowing red jewelled eyes, are early Victorian, the Queen herself having had a gold serpent engagement ring set with

Four nineteenth century rings. The marquise ring of diamonds is late Victorian; the turquoise and gold with pendant heart is early Victorian; the cluster set in gold is mid-Victorian and the garnet flower, set in gold, is the earliest, in a late Victorian box.

137

emeralds. Heraldic and ecclesiastical patterns are also early Victorian. One of the most delightful rings in this type carries a vinaigrette on a chain. Queen Victoria owned a blue enamel ring set in gold and decorated with a few small pearls. Attached to it was a fine gold chain on which was suspended the egg-shaped vinaigrette. Another ring, with an enamelled vinaigrette ornamented with a bunch of white flowers held together with pink ribbons, is suspended on to a ring by a heavy looking gold chain which has links decorated with dark blue enamel and tiny flowers of paler blue.

Ivy leaves, coral hands, flowers and single stone rings, as well as those shaped like a belt with a buckle and serpents, following the Queen's choice, are circa 1840 to 1845. Three or four coiled serpents and the strap and buckle ring were still in favour in the 1890's, so dating is not very easy. A half-hoop of pearls was another design much in favour for engagement rings, with fine disregard for their symbolism of tears. Favourite gems included turquoise, garnet, rubies and emeralds and also coral. A very desirable little ring of sentiment is known as a 'regard' ring, in which the stones spell out the word or sometimes they spell 'dearest'.

Mid-Victorian rings dating from about 1860 to 1880 in everyday use were comparatively inexpensive and the fashionable 'gipsy' ring with a diamond, a ruby or a sapphire set very deep into the gold, came into vogue towards 1875. Pearls or diamonds were customary for engagement rings, whilst the 'Keeper' was a gold ring without any stones. It was engraved or chased. There were, of course, very fine expensive rings too, set with enormous stones and engraved by a master craftsman or else enamelled. One amusing design of this period was the handkerchief ring. On the wedding-ring finger, with its plain gold 'Keeper', a ring was worn with a larger ring attached, through which a suitably gossamer handkerchief could be slipped. The Etruscan and Greek, Byzantine and geometrical patterns were 'in' and all those insects, serpents, swans and other birds, butterflies, stars and sphinxes as well. Initials, monograms and mottoes were also the mode in jewellery and we find good quality enamel, cable twists and pendant fringes on jewellery of this date. The attractive tortoiseshell pieces inlaid with patterns in gold and silver are circa 1865. Coloured gold was much in use and in second-class jewellery settings were of plain or oxidized or imitation silver and of steel as well as low carat and imitation gold.

Late Victorian rings, from circa 1885, have those charming two- and three-part rings, marquise rings, two rows of stones and hearts; gipsy rings are still in fashion and single stone diamonds are set in a very narrow band of gold. Wedding rings began to get narrower about 1890, but it must have always been a little bit a question of personal taste, as many girls married in early Edwardian days had wide heavy gold wedding rings.

A catalogue of The Goldsmiths' and Silversmiths' Company dated 1900 shows a page of contemporary rings, all costing under £25, and some designs obviously remained popular for years, including the diamond cluster round a find pearl on a plain gold band and the cross-over ring set with a diamond and a pearl. In fact all the rings on one page are diamonds and pearl-set, with the exception of an occasional ruby.

For collectors perhaps the best advice to give them is to buy what they like. Then changing tastes and fashions will not affect them. It goes without saying that good workmanship and design, together with undamaged materials, are essential.

SILVER

I
Miniature 'Toys'

Anybody interested in antiques sooner or later comes up against the sad truth that he has to choose between specialization and diversity. There is much to be said on either side. The specialist in one line will have a far greater and deeper knowledge of his subject than the impulsive discoverer of more and more fresh fields to explore. Interesting new facts about the specialist's choice will be a source of great satisfaction to him, and to know a great deal about one matter means that the expert will seldom be cheated and will often find new examples of his chosen object where the less knowledgeable person would have missed them or not recognised them.

Lady Bracknell asked Ernest Worthing if he knew everything or nothing and was satisfied when he said, 'I know nothing, Lady Bracknell.' Perhaps to know a little about a lot of things nevertheless has some advantages. It probably all depends on the temperament of individuals. One thing a collector cannot do without is that natural inborn flair, which gradually develops into a sixth sense, like Macbeth's witch's 'by the pricking of my thumbs', and tells him that the object he has just picked out of a tray of rubbish is 'right'. We all have had our small successes to balance against the failures. That 17th century silver and enamelled acorn pomander that looked like tin until we examined it at home under a magnifying glass; or the dirty little black cream jug half an inch high that turned miraculously into an 18th century 'toy' when treated with a silver-dip product. On the other side of the coin, do not be discouraged to find that the splendid silver cake-basket the size of a gooseberry was made in 1908 and not in 1808 as you had supposed, and moreover you paid the price of an early one for it. After all there is always tomorrow, and the inveterate collector never stops searching.

Monsieur Henri d'Allemagne, who was a noted antiquarian but belonged to the class of collector who is extremely catholic in taste, never let a day pass, according to his son, when he did not bring a treasure home to add to his hoard. Amongst other things he was passionately interested in toys, in both senses of the word, and what remained of his huge collection was mouth-watering to see a few years ago. Miniature silver, tiny pieces of furniture, dolls, toys, games from very far back in history, and rooms full of large furniture and other treasures of all descriptions as well.

In the past royal children were often sent toys from other royal families across Europe. The Pope sent little coaches and soldiers and other silver miniatures to King John of Poland's children in 1683. As these small masterpieces were still in existence in Poland in the 1920's presumably they were not treated as toys in the customary sense of the word but treasured as 'toys' in the earlier meaning. Henry II of France's daughter ordered a set of silver toys in 1576 which included 'buffet pots', bowls and plates and other little gems which were sent as a gift to the Duchess of Bavaria's children. No doubt they too were only allowed to enjoy such expensive playthings if their governess was present.

There was a goldsmith called John Sotro, who was flourishing circa 1740–50. His trade-card can be seen in the British Museum.

Miniature teapot, coffee pot and cream jug, en suite,
mid-19th century.

He would have had for sale such tableware as tea pots, coffee pots and chocolate pots as well as buttons, buckles, vinaigrettes and snuff-boxes. Miniature candlesticks, four tiny salt-cellars and a pair of sauce boats bear his mark. Toymen were making dolls' house furniture in England from about 1665 and luckily many were hall-marked. I believe there are at least fifty silver 'toys' in the Westbrook baby house. As this architectural gem remained in the same family for about 250 years the contents were not dispersed. Not only was the small silver marked but it bore proudly the compulsory Britannia with the lion's head erased which was used on the high standard silver used in the period between 1697 and 1720. Toymen known to have made this sort of small silver in the 18th century are men like Jonah Clifton, who registered his mark at Goldsmiths' Hall in 1708; Matthew Madden registered as early as 1696; and George Middleton, 1684's. Edward Medleycott entered in 1748.

David Clayton was another famous toyman working at the beginning of the 18th century, who entered Goldsmiths' Hall in 1720. Sir Charles Oman found that the mark A.C. on miniatures that had been previously attributed to Augustine Courtauld was in fact D.C. and the mark of David Clayton. He also made the point that 'English silver toys are always utensils'. This was of course distinct from the Dutch 'toys' which included little sets of soldiers, figures, horses and carriages, even acrobats.

Besides all the exquisite little tableware pieces there were also fireplaces complete with fire irons and fenders, candle-sconces and warming pans. Mr. Delieb[1] reminds us that some of these toys, marked only with the maker's initials, were not for sale but were used as travellers' samples in the days when highwaymen, and other thieves were a very real hazard on every journey.

It is as well to remember that early in the 19th century some miniature tableware was being made very much smaller than the 17th and 18th century ones which were about two inches high. These are not often carrying either date or maker's mark, being comparatively thin and light.

---

[1] *Investing in Silver* by Eric Delieb. Barrie and Rockcliff, 1967.

Some other small silver

A very pretty fashion of early and mid-Victorian times was the posy-holder, which a lady going to a ball, a reception or a dinner-party would carry in her gloved hand. It would be filled with a small bunch of scented flowers and some were made with a pin to fasten on the corsage. They are very elegant and pretty little bygones and most collectable. They are to be found in many materials, but the best are of gold, silver or filigree, sometimes with mother-of-pearl handles, sometimes set with precious or semi-precious stones and occasionally fitted with a reducing mirror from which the people behind can be viewed discreetly when held in the right position.

The cast silver ones are beautifully chased, and they are often shapes like a cornucopia. I have two unusual examples, one of very good quality which is in trumpet form and holds the bouquet

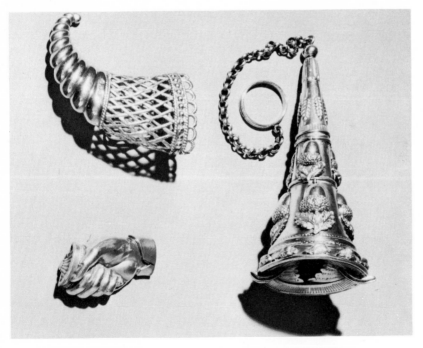

Rare cornucopia posy holder by Joseph Willmore, 1836, Birmingham; another rare posy-holder with patent fitting by B H J embossed with acorns and leaves. A miniature hand posy-holder, Mid-19th century.

in a tight grip when the necessary catch is pressed. The other one is also silver and in the shape of a miniature hand. This is fitted with a pin to fix on the ample bosom of a late Victorian lady.

Silver thimbles, and silver-gilt ones too, are to be found dating from the 16th century. Early ones have tent-shaped tops and their rims are often inscribed with some charming motto. This fashion also is a feature of the 18th century ones and also early in Queen Victoria's reign. The owner used sometimes to have her name engraved on the rim. Mid-18th century thimbles have bands with scrolls, flowers or crests engraved on them. One clue as to date is the long high domed shape of the early ones and the fact that Victorian thimbles were often engraved with some view of a famous church or bridge, as they were very suitable souvenir gifts. The silver thimbles made from 1739 until 1790 were never hall-

A Victorian silver chatelaine, hall-marked and dated 1877. It is rare to find one with all its original pieces. Also, two silver posy-holders, mid-19th century.

144

marked, but all through the 19th century until 1890 the duty stamp of the monarch's head was always included in the hall-mark. Another piece of small silver that was always marked in England was the tobacco tamper.

Spoons are very collectable small silver, and they conjure up fascinating customs like the first introduction of tea, when mote-skimmers were used. These elegant perforated spoons with leafy or geometric patterns usually have a point at the end of the handles, though I have seen one with a marrow scoop on the end of it. They are generally supposed to have been used to skim floating tea-leaves off the surface of the pale tea in the small handleless tea-bowls of the first tea sets. The point is believed to be either for clearing the teapot spout so that it pours properly, or, rather less credibly, to spear lemon-pips. Tea strainers were a later development first appearing towards the very end of the 18th century. Caddy-spoons are already being collected by a discerning Society and these are in a great variety of shapes.

Medicine spoons could add a slightly sinister note to a collection. For instance the early 19th century and 18th century covered spoons for administering caster-oil are beautifully made, some with a hole at the end of the handle which, when closed by the thumb, had the effect of keeping the deadly potion in the spoon, until it was safely in the victim's mouth. The operative end also had a hole of course.

Another Georgian medicine spoon had a large spoon one end and a small one the other, presumably for different sized doses.

In a less painful vein there are marrow spoons or scoops, and children's spoons, even as early as 1640 complete with slip-top terminal. There are beautiful varieties of tea spoons, salt spoons and snuff spoons as well. The aristocrats of a collection of spoons are the Apostle spoons of Henry VIII's reign and the Maidenhead spoons with a girl's head terminal; also the Apostle spoons of later dates until they disappeared some time in the middle of the 17th century. These antique spoons and the Stuart cast terminal spoons are not only lovely in themselves but to explore their history is a very worthwhile study that would repay any collector. Apostle spoons can be misleading to the beginner, though, as 20th century ones are not difficult to find.

Recently a local market stall proved to be a little treasure-trove of small silver. It yielded a pocket corkscrew, with a handle of mother-of-pearl which is marked with an oblong shield enclosing the initials IT, probably, therefore, Joseph Taylor and dated early 19th century at latest. There was an oval mother-of-pearl magnifying glass mounted in silver of the same date and a strange table nutmeg grater that could possibly be mounted in the 'German silver' invented about 1830 by Samuel Roberts, who replaced copper foundation metal for plated silver with this white alloy. He used an ornate scrolling Rococo style of design which had returned to fashion about 1830. One of the greatest amusements for a collector is in the pursuit of an attribution.

Corkscrews were first of all called augers and then the rod was made straight. From the mid-17th century the spiral was invented and in Pepy's day he would have called it a bottle-screw. Miniature corkscrews were made for opening toilet waters and scent bottles and these were spiralled their whole length. Pocket corkscrews, like my market stall discovery, fitting into a detachable silver sheath, did not appear until 1750. Corkscrews were often included in *étuis* or in picnic sets in Georgian days. Very few small pocket ones were made after the 1830's.

III

Wine-drinking accessories

Silver wine labels, sometimes called bottle tickets, date from the 18th century, the earliest being after 1725. There are innumerable designs to be found, and as they are small and extremely decorative a good collection of these would be a worthwhile hobby. The initials are very handsome. Many designs naturally favour a grape and vine motif, sometimes including Bacchus being offered a glass by a cupid. An amusing set with hounds standing on the letters of the wines, sherry, madeira, port and claret, must surely have a belonged to some sporting Regency character, unless it is a family crest. Hester Bateman made these little labels and other members of this famous goldsmith family. They are made in enamel as well.

There is something very elegant about a beautiful cut glass decanter dressed with a splendid silver label made by one of our well-known silversmiths. One must however remember that originally they hung much less grandly round the shoulders of those roughly made wine-bottles of the mid-18th century. Then, of course, they were called bottle tickets and only became glorified as 'decanter labels' many years later. It is a fascinating social study to look for all the strange names on wine labels. We will find some very odd drinks indeed, like shrub, arrack, constantia, nig, frontignac and vidonia. Mrs. Jennings, in *Sense and Sensibility* offered Marianne a glass of 'the finest old Constantia wine in the house that ever was tasted', which her husband had been so fond of when he had a 'touch of his old colicky gout'. In this case it was offered to mend a breaking heart.

Shrub was a drink made from acid fruits, sugar and spirits. Arrack was a spirit distilled from coconut and vidonia was the name given to a dry white wine made in the Canaries.

Sack, which we now call sherry, is constantly mentioned in Shakespeare's comedies. Even earlier Chaucer refers to 'clarrie'. Dr. Andrew Borde[1], a distinguished physician whose book about diet and health was published in the reign of Edward I, wrote, '. . . all the kingdoms of the world have not so many sundry kinds of wines as be in England, and yet there is nothing to make wine of.' The significance of this remark was that we never have made good wine in England despite every effort. The rich man's table has always been stocked with wines from sunnier countries like France, Italy, Spain and Greece. Our own wines were never considered good enough for the Court. The cheap produce from the monks' vineyards is believed to have been intended for culinary use as vinegar, or for the domestic staff to drink or for offering to the poor man at the gate. Cider and ale were quite another matter. We have always been famous for these homely drinks for centuries. There may not be wine labels for them, but beer has been provided with a fine coaster which would have been used at an inn where the leather black-jack would have stood in company with a tankard. In the example I have seen, however, the coaster was made of oak with a brass rim inscribed, 'Breakfast with health, Dine with Contentment'. Its date is about 1820.

However, in spite of out lack of the proper climate for harvesting good grapes, our housewives have been very enterprising over home made cheer. *The Compleat Housewife* of 1753 describes how

---

[1]See *The Pleasure of your Company* by Jean Latham.

to make 'Frontiniac Wine'. The French version, Frontenac was a muscat wine. The English version used raisins, sugar, elderflowers, syrup of lemon and ale yeast. Whether this is the one our silver bottle label would have graced is a moot point. *The Compleat Housewife* also gives a receipe for 'the fine Clary Wine' which is certainly not claret. Those whites of 12 eggs and that 25 pounds of sugar boiled gently for an hour are put with a herb called clary, or *Salvia Sclarea* and goodness knows what that can have tasted like. Could it have been what Chaucer meant by 'clarrie'?

Shelley's friend Captain Gronow, who published some volumes of recollections of his life at 'Court, the Camp and the Clubs' in the early 19th century, tells us that the fashionable wines then were port, sherry and hock, 'claret and even Burgundy being then designated poor, thin, washy stuff'. He adds that as soon as diners, both men and women, had tasted their soup 'from that moment everybody was taking wine with everybody else till the close of dinner; and such wine as produced that class of cordiality which frequently wanders into stupefaction.'

This little digression into the past shows how fascinating the pursuit of antique collecting can be, leading as it does into the byways of social history. Before leaving wine-labels, it is worth remembering the ornaments which date periods. For instance, the plain crescents and rectangles are from the 1730's, followed by feather-edging from about 1740 and the piercings and crestings begin circa 1770; then embossing starts in the 1790's. Plain labels, rectangular with clipped off corners went on being popular for many years. Oval labels, and after them a pointed oval, are the 1770's and 1780's. In the 19th century by 1825 vine leaves appear with perforated lettering. This is only a very perfunctory guide and collectors need good books specializing in the subject, as well as a really good reliable dealer to help them.

Other accessories to drinking in the small silver class are those lovely toddy ladles, usually matching the punch-bowls, which can be found with circular or oval escallop shell bowls and handles of silver, hardwood, whalebone and ivory. Pouring lips were often made to make easier the serving of the 'pale puntz, vulgarly known by the name of punch', as Thomas Worlidge wrote in 1675.

There are of course coasters, used to protect the shining

mahogany tables from stains, and these appear from about 1760. The earliest ones were all silver but from 1775 onwards the boxwood bases were being used. The decanter stands were of course wider and not so tall in the rim as bottle stands. If you find a double coaster, this will not be dated earlier than 1790.

An odd piece of silver whose use may defeat the uninitiated is a toddy-lifter. This was a rather complicated method of getting the toddy into the glass by means of a long thin tube ending in a bottle shaped container with a hole at the bottom of it. Plunged into the drink, the liquid enters the hole at the base and when it is full the server puts his thumb over the hole in the neck or tube and creates a vacuum. This enables him to raise the toddy-lifter out of the punch-bowl and then, on releasing his thumb, the toddy pours into the glass. The ladle seems an easier method of serving today, but it certainly gives variety to the ceremony.

Small silver of good quality is always collected and even a selection of about forty little 'toys', mostly dating to the turn of the century, which were chiefly tables, chairs and small figures, fetched £465 at auction early in 1971.

TOYS

I

Many Inventions

In Kent's London Directory of 1738 three 'toymen' are listed; William Deard, Frederick Deveer and Thoman Wildey. In 1754 these three were still in the Directory and Coles Child was added to the list. Even earlier, in 1720, Defoe mentioned a toyshop in Edinburgh; but of course these toys were trinkets like buttons or shoe-buckles or miniature pieces of silver. 'I had an entire set of silver dishes and plates,' says Gulliver, when he visited Brobdingnag, adding, '. . . they were not much bigger than what I have seen of the same kind in a London toyshop for the furniture of a baby house.' In the same category were the chess and domino sets, cup-and-ball toys and the little carved animals all made to the same tiny scale. Edmund Burke (1728–92) called Birmingham 'the toyshop of Europe', probably referring to their small silver articles like buckles and buttons.

A hundred years or so later Watkins' London Directories of 1852–5 listed a number of doll-makers and at the same time there appeared other lists, quite separate from the dolls, of toy manufacturers in the modern sense of the word. The famous Pierotti family arrived in England about 1793 and began making their beautiful wax dolls at the Pantheon in Oxford Street, continuing this labour of love right up until the 1930's. The Montanari family were not so long in business, starting in Regent Street in 1849 and carrying on until 1886, doing wax-modelling as well as making dolls.

Another Directory of 1868 listed toy manufacturers who imported and exported toys, china, games like cricket and archery as well as board games, jewellery, clocks, musical boxes and dolls, all of which goods came under the umbrella term of toys. In 1891 toy-makers were advertising 'seaside pails, drums, watercans etc.', and one was offering 'pitch pine carts and horses'. A pull-along horse of carved wood which is realistically covered in hide is dated circa 1880 and can be seen in the London Museum where many other delightful toys are on show. They have a clockwork walking dog covered in pale brown kid, circa 1885, an American wooden doll on a clockwork tricycle, dated about 1870, and a delightfully primitive train set of painted wood which was sold in its chip box complete with wooden track, made in Germany about 1845. Another American doll is the 'Autoperipatetikos' which walks after being wound up by a key and also dates circa 1870. Clockwork toys began to be mass produced as early as 1850, but earlier mechanical devices like trickling sand and magnetism are also represented in this museum. One remarkable negro soldier, made around 1870, dances from a wire attached to his back which jerks up and down when a drum below is filled with water and a night-light flame is lit beneath so that steam from a little funnel spins a wheel to operate the dancer. This was presumably not a toy to be played with by children on their own.

Toys naturally belong in this book as they are nearly all miniature versions of objects we all use in everyday life, or else miniature versions of human beings and animals, houses, shops, stables, circuses and even churches. Noah's arks are said to have their origin in the 16th century at Oberammergau, but the ones we can occasionally find for sale and certainly see in toy museums, mostly date to the 19th century. Not only animals inhabit these delightful arks, but also outsize insects like grasshoppers, butterflies and beetles that stand, with splendid disregard for scale, shoulder to shoulder with elephants, giraffes and camels. These toys probably survive in comparatively good condition because they were the only toy allowed to children on Victorian Sundays. By the 1880's the figures of Noah and his family are sometimes found wearing clothes of soft material and occasionally fashionable Victorian beards.

Animals have always been popular toys, from rocking-horses, one version of which is in the London Museum[1] said to be over 300 years old, to pull along horses, oxen, dogs, goats and donkeys

[1] Mary Hillier in *Pageant of Toys* shows a similar one which is German, made about the end of the 18th century.

with or without carts attached to them. Stick or hobby-horses
with heads did not appear until the 15th century, according to
Mr. Patrick Murray of the enchanting Museum of Childhood in
Edinburgh. The true hobby-horse shown in his book called *Toys*
is a mediaeval looking horse wearing a flowing coat which hides
the rider's legs. The child gets into an opening in the saddle and
canters about on his own legs. It looks much more realistic and
satisfying than the rather painful stick-horse.

Toys for the bath or water do not seem to have appeared much
until the beginning of the 19th century and then they never lost
favour, particularly the ducks. One very attractive example of this
genre is the eggshell bisque swan which is as light as a feather and
floats gracefully on the water, though not many can have survived
from their birth in Germany circa 1880. They also make charming
table decorations in a glass bowl with a few flower heads and leaves.
In the 17th century they would have been swimming on tiny lakes
fed by cascades of water moved by heat or hand-pumps and con-

A mid-19th century horse and cart. The horse is covered
in hide and is 12 inches high at its head.

trolled by magnets. Go to Paris and see the *Musée des Arts et Métiers* for examples of early mechanical toys for children of all ages.

The clockwork pictures, which are little animated landscapes sometimes with musical boxes attached, are quite irresistible. The early ones of the 17th and 18th centuries can only be seen in museums; but once they reached the nursery in about the middle of the 19th century, they are less rare even though far less desirable. We can still find the fiddler cat and her kittens and the little boy sticking out his tongue at the photographer, both accompanied by creaking music. Others sold a few years ago were three cats somersaulting on ladders with two others dancing and others looking on; and a miller blowing the windmill by a bellows, then stopping for a drink from his bottle, his wife shouting at him from the house and another miller waving from the mill. Both of these are in picture-frame glazed cases. Animated scenes under glass domes could also be found a few years ago without much difficulty. Ships toss on the sea with a lighthouse and Gothic church, the tower is inset with a watch movement; a musical base has another ship near a tower and a Zouave sentry is marching round; a gallant company of cavalry marches across a bridge to the sound of music, there is a windmill, a clock tower and a mill wheel all in action.

Mechanical toys are probably most popular with boys, and they are collected by adults just as avidly as are dolls and dolls' houses at present. The clown with a troublesome bucking donkey to drive is made of gaily decorated tin-plate and was found recently in its original box. It was made by a German firm called Lehmann in about 1910. Another German tinplate toy was the scissor-grinder who, on being wound, feverishly sharpens his pair of scissors by a treadle device and the sparks fly from the little piece of iron pyrite attached to the stone. One French clockwork toy by Fernand Martin animates a barber polishing his bald-headed customer's pate with a very unsuccessful hair-restorer. These are all examples of our world in miniature and even in action. One reason they are collected is for the social history they tell. You can follow the story of the train, the car, the aeroplane and even architecture, shops and clothes in the world of toys.

Magic lanterns are one of the most out-of-date toys nowadays in this our television-cum-cinema society. They date from the late 18th century, but of course their disadvantages are obviously their poor illumination and the bad glass that was used. However, by the 1890's they had improved considerably and with slipping, moveable and rackwork slides they could give the illusion of movement.

The magical little translucent scenes in the Panorama Panoptique is another example of the toy world imitating life. These are quite rare and difficult to photograph. They are contained in a green box with six pictures and these are viewed in turn through a bellows which can simulate day or night effects by opening at the back or the top. A view of the Thames tunnel is one of the most popular pictures, but often there are French scenes as this was a French invention.

Another toy much in demand just at present is the American cast iron money-box. There are many different models which have been in production since 1875 until about 1920 and indeed there are at least 300 different mechanical Banks. British ones were made between 1890 and 1914. One of the best is William Tell shooting the apple off his son's head. It is marked 'patented June 23, 1896'. The famous 'Tammany Bank' one is a portrait of William 'Boss' Tweed seated in his red chair, wearing a nice yellow waistcoat. He slips the coins put into his hand straight into his pocket. This notorious character was chairman of the Tammany Hall political party. He gained control of the financial affairs of New York, robbing it of a small fortune, until he was arrested in 1871.

The difference between 17th and 18th century children and those born in the early 19th century was that before 1800 they were dressed and looked upon as miniature adults, given comparatively few toys, unless they came from rich homes, and treated with affection but also with considerable severity. By the end of the 18th century they were considered simply as immature creatures that must eventually take their place in the adult world. By 1800 there was the beginning of a new outlook of indulgence within the framework of a vengeful religion, which nevertheless gave the children a rock of security to lean upon for the rest of their lives.

From 1800 onwards a flood of toys invaded the child's world and it is these fascinating little models of everyday things that adults, with true 18th century zeal, collect, date, research and hoard in

154

their display cabinets today. Hoarding up these little pieces of history is a national hobby now and any beginners had better start their collections before it is too late. The forgers are already at work in any field where prices are rising and cast-iron banks are being copied as well as Parisienne dolls.

II

Shops, Rooms and Kitchens

Playing houses and playing shops or hospitals or farmers, or for that matter playing soldiers are, all unknowingly to the child, a way of learning how to live in the grown-up world. A thirty-year-old doctor friend used to play with my daughter a game of hospitals when they were both about six years old. A large vegetable marrow was the patient and a trap-door was cut in its middle and a good bundle of string secreted inside for 'operations'. One day the 'doctor' lost his temper over an unsuccessful operation, the 'patient' was bundled unceremoniously out of the window and another occupation had to be found. A similar game of hospitals was played by one of my contemporaries and her brother towards the end of the First World War. In this case their scale was smaller. The family dolls' house was converted into a hospital for convalescent soldiers and the small dolls bandaged up and put to bed. This took care of many long afternoons and a lot of hard work was put into the painting and converting of the dolls' house, the making of blue uniforms for convalescent soldiers and the manufacturing of beds from cigar boxes.

Continental children could be given devotional toys and in the early 1900's little wooden altars were to be found in the shops, complete with tin candlesticks, bells, holy water sprinklers and so forth. Dolls' *prie-dieus* might even have a musical box beneath to add a few notes of religious music to give the extra touch of reality to the game. Of course there were Christmas crèches too in miniature sizes.

Stables satisfied the boys and could be bought ready boxed with the various horses, a wagonette and handcart and even a ladder, as well as all the accessories needed by well cared for horses.

Dolls' shops are not easy to find now, partly perhaps because the little miniscule fittings were too tempting both to the owner and her friends, who would want to take them out of their setting

Miniature doll's house (14 inches by 10½ inches) containing peg-wooden dolls, all *c.* 1830–4, in contemporary clothes. The furnishings are mid-19th century.

This delightful and rare fishmonger's shop (*c.* 1840) is
similar to the better known butcher's shop.
(Courtesy of Rupert Gentle)

so that they were lost or destroyed. The dolls' shops, which were
often models and not playthings, have survived intact more often
and we find the butcher's shop, the fishmonger and the *modiste*
occasionally. Here again is a miniature piece of history, a painting
or photograph come to frozen life in three dimensions.

From about 1880 a splendid dolls' kitchen stove reached the
shops to glamourize cooking in the minds of children. The oven
doors opened, the copper pans, kettle and fish-kettle with its tap,
were all of excellent quality and a small device working on oil
could be lit to heat saucepans and ovens. The Germans were still
making their traditional 'Nuremberg kitchens', only of metal
instead of wood, in 1900. Mr. Patrick Murray points out that
these were in fact 17th century Dutch 'domestic science toys' and

157

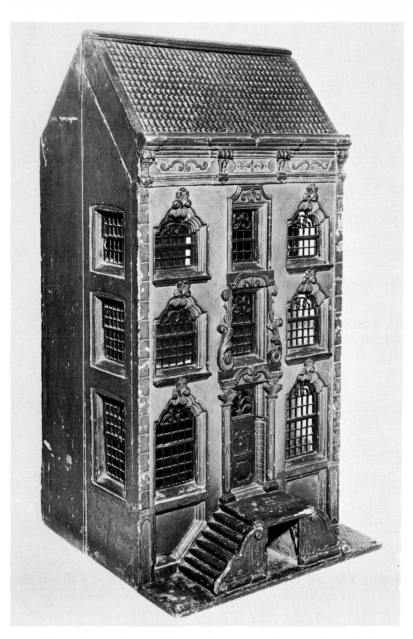

Typical town house that can be seen in Amsterdam. This
baby house dates between 1680 and 1710.

(Courtesy of Celia Haynes and family)

two very old ladies I know own a magnificent Dutch example, dating to the end of the 17th century, which is made of oak and filled with a treasure store of miniature kitchen requirements.[1] The Bethnal Green Museum has an example of a 17th century kitchen in a baby house of this period.

In 1870 the Americans had the cunning idea of making tiny dummies of shop goods, thus pleasing children and advertising their brands of soup, cereals, coffees, teas and so forth in one easy movement. Later, about 1904, samples of miniature size with eatables or drinkables inside appeared. These lasted for at least thirty years and in about 1920 I remember how mortified I was when a small friend eat up all the sweets in the bottles of my sweetshop, so the tiny scales and cone-shaped bags were useless.

Besides the model butcher and fish shops of about the 1840's there were, a little earlier, shops which had been made purely as toys and not for instruction as to the different joints or fish available. These have a Noah's ark quality which is endearing and their complete unreality takes away from their rather painful subject. The Victorians with Germanic thoroughness did not scruple to emphasize the dripping blood and sharp knife in the butcher's model shops. Greengrocer shops are less lurid and in the Tunbridge Wells Museum there is a splendid greengrocery market stall complete with fruit, vegetables, eggs and even hens for sale, as well as a very exceptional fish market stall with crabs, shell fish and baskets of sea-food on sale beautifully decorated with pieces of seaweed.

Pedlar dolls have always fascinated the lover of miniature things but alas so many have been 'restored'.

As with the dolls' shops, 20th century children, less inhibited than their parents and grandparents were, took off the pedlar's trays many of the tiny wares and we are the poorer now. Excellently made modern pedlar dolls are being made by hand which could well be collectors' pieces of the future. But mostly these are pastiches of the old ones; and indeed they could hardly be anything else as there are virtually no pedlars today, though just before the 1939 War there were still traders standing in busy London streets and

---

[1] See *Dolls Houses* by Jean Latham for fuller description.

selling fairground types of toys, mostly from the Continent, like the wooden traditional hens pecking imaginary grain, German mechanical toys and jumping furry animals at the end of elastic strings, and glasses of water gay with diminutive Japanese paper flowers that are transformed from dull little screwed up pieces into beautiful bunches of flowers when the water has touched them.

III

Games

Games can sometimes be found in true miniature size. Cup-and-ball or bilboquet, familiar in 16th century France and right up to Victorian times, is charming in its tiny 18th century version, when it is made of ivory or bone, and the long wooden cups that look like a flower on a tapering stalk are also attractive. Prisoners-of-war in Napoleonic times made delightful boxes in bone, filled with handmade dominoes, the lids marked as a cribbage board. Full size boards are sometimes included in a box for playing cards and these often have almost invisible sliding lids over a small indentation that holds the marked pegs. There are 18th century ones about and the inlaid wooden ones were a speciality of Tunbridge, says Mr. Pinto[1], making the point that inlay is distinct from mosaic. Cribbage boards are quite a study in themselves and come in many different shapes and sizes. Incidentally cribbage is an excellent card game for two and the fact that it dates back to the early 17th century gives it an extra interest to those of us who enjoy searching and probing into origins and historical details.

Dice cubes are also very early toys, more used perhaps by adults in their gambling games than by children. I have a small ormolu cube marked with the customary dots from 1 to 6 in tiny pearls. One side of the cube, which is about a quarter of an inch in height, width and breadth, opens to reveal inside two even smaller dice made of metal. A two inch ebony box also contains three dice, and this is presumably 19th century. Dice have been found in ancient Egyptian tombs, so their history is worth looking into as well.

[1] *Treen and Other Wooden Bygones* by Edward H. Pinto.

Miniature dolls' house (14 x 10 inches) containing
peg-wooden dolls, all c 1830-40 in contemporary
clothes and furnishings mostly mid-nineteenth century.

Photo by Studio Wreford

Dominoes in sliding-lid boxes are often to be found and they date from the days of Queen Anne. There should be 28 pieces to make a set. Besides the prisoner-of-war ones already mentioned there are many other attractive boxes for dominoes in various woods and ivory and bone. One very attractive one is Eskimo—made in the early 19th century in the shape of a seal. Its back forms the lid.

Solitaire boards are older than you might expect, coming to us from the Continent in the 18th century; these early ones have no runnel for the discarded marbles and they are not highly polished like the 19th century ones. I have never seen a miniature one,

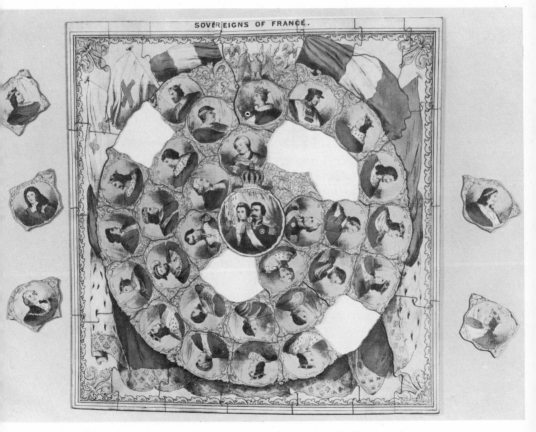

This is an example of that maddening type of dissected puzzle that has to be assembled before the game of 'Sovereigns of France' can be played. *c.* 1855.

L

though they were made in several sizes. Their charm lies in the lovely French marbles of circa 1840, which should grace the mid-Victorian ones.

Miniature chess sets are rare and when they do turn up they are seldom in perfect condition. Their tiny size, to fit a dolls' house, is not easily photographed. Chess sets also come in various sizes, from travelling sets to splendid pieces that can be seen in the Victoria and Albert Museum, to give but one example. They are made in all sorts of materials, semi-precious stones, silver, brass and bronze, pewter, porcelain and pottery, glass and perhaps most commonly of bone, ivory or wood. The largest one, which is shown in Mr. Pinto's book on Treen, is gigantic. The kings are 12 inches high and they stand on a four-legged table marked as a chess-board. You could hardly find a wider contrast between this enormous early 17th century set and my dolls' house example which has pieces scarcely higher than a capital letter in this book.

Besides the cup-and-ball game, which was played out of doors, there are miniature ninepin sets, carpet bowls of pottery in gay patterns and table croquet sets. In 1661 Samuel Pepys played the early form of croquet, then called pele-mele or pall-mall, with the Duke of York. They played it in St. James's Park and Pepys noted that it was 'the first time that ever I played the sport'. The small table croquet sets in boxes, with a green cloth to spread over and protect the table, were in fashion from about 1850, when the game in its present form was introduced over here.

Spillikins is another game with a long history and its tiny bone, ivory of wooden pieces are carved into various shapes with numbers on them. The game is to remove one spillikin or spellican from the hundred or so thrown at random into a pile. On no account must any other spillikin move or the turn is forfeited to the next player. This game has been played in England since the early 18th century but its origin is believed to have been in China centuries ago. My own set came in an odd wooden box shaped like a cigar and has two bone hooks for players to whisk the pieces dexterously off the heap.

Playing-cards exercise a very special appeal to some collectors. Well-known before A.D. 1000 in Asia, they were handmade originally and were beautifully painted and illuminated. When they were established in Europe about the end of the 14th century they were used exclusively by royalty and courtiers, a game very much for the aristocracy. However, it did not take long for a kind of mass-production to develop, so that, after another 100 years had passed, more people were enjoying this addicting pastime. There is a walnut card-table at Hardwick Hall inlaid with playing-cards, that art of *trompe l'oeil* being hundreds of years old. In the Lateran Museum in Rome, for instance, there is the *Unswept Floor* mosaic, which comes from Greco-Roman times, vividly conjuring up the debris left after a feast.

That discriminating French collector and historian Henry-René d'Allemagne wrote a book called *Les Cartes à Jouer du XIV ème au XX ème Siecle* in 1906, a two-volume study which is now a collectors' piece in its own right. If you consider that in 1754 in only one province of France they produced more than 200,000 packs, the immensity of the study of this subject is quickly apparent.

A few years ago, travelling in France, we chanced upon an antiques fair in a church, of all places. Here I found a handful of cards with two Kings and two Jacks, which were the standard 'plumed' Jacks made in 18th century Auvergne and Burgundy. They had later been used by a notary to mark his clients' files, for on their backs were names. One was 'Roudil—(Sébastien) Tangier' and beneath this a capital C and 'Roche, Dufayet'. On the back of another card a note was scribbled about a legacy to the curé of some church. What a splendid start for a novel of adventure and intrigue. Handmade cards soon became too dirty and greasy to play with and then the owners either used them for notes, or for visiting-cards or, as in the above case, to mark files of names. These old cards are not easy to find for obvious reasons.

Today there are five different standard packs of cards used in France. During the 18th century there were over a dozen. Tarot cards are the earliest European ones, with their flavour of magic and romance. There are 78 cards in a pack and they were used for telling fortunes and are reproduced today in their old form complete with a book of information about the formula for reading the future. This is of course a game universally popular which has never palled over the years.

Identities of the figures on cards cause a lot of headaches to collectors. French cards certainly came to England and were

163

L*

adapted to our own use, but it is at least doubtful whether Henry VIII is portrayed as the King of Hearts, as similar kings holding an axe appeared all over France and Spain at that time. The French Court cards were and still are named as a rule. Charles, the King of Hearts is believed to have represented Charlemagne; the King of Spades, called David, is probably the biblical one; the Jack of Clubs is Lancelot. As Charles I granted a Charter to the Worshipful Company of Makers of Playing Cards in 1628, this shows how well established they were by the early 17th century and gives us some idea of the complexity of collecting old cards. But as with any other hobby, the more we study the subject the more fascinating and absorbing it becomes.

The costumes of English playing cards date from Tudor times and all our Queens were variations of Henry VIII's mother, Elizabeth of York, hence the white rose she always carries. The knaves, with square hat, 'petticote' and long covering coat like a dressing gown, wearing the fashionable clothes of a court dandy of the period, remain virtually unchanged to this day.

The artists who drew the court cards, which, by the way, were originally called coat cards, worked first on illuminated manuscripts and their beautiful gilding and bold colours have seldom been bettered. Lucky is the collector who finds these sought-after early cards mounted on parchment.

As for the games themselves, in its early form whist was played by Henry VIII, but rummy is probably even older. Columbus's seamen played a variant called 'âs-nâs', taught to them, so it is said, by the sailors of Cathay. Charles IX of France played another version called 'gilet' and remarked piously, after the massacre of St. Bartholomew: 'At gilet this day I lost my purse, but at St. Bartholomew I lost my soul'.

The 17th century was a great period for gambling and the famous games of faro, trente-et-quarante and baccarat were the vogue. In the 18th and 19th centuries the fashionable games were ombre and piquet. Quite a sharp line was drawn between games played by the nobility and those enjoyed by lesser mortals. The clergy, for instance, stuck to whist, whereas the man in the street preferred a jolly game of all-fours or cribbage.

A private collector owns a pack of 17th century cards illustrating various incidents in the Great Fire of London, the Popish Plot

18th century cards found in a notary's client's files.
Note the name written on the back and also the names
César, La Hire, etc.

and other exciting events of the times. The card for the Knave
of Spades shows the unlucky Sir E. Godfrey being followed by
conspirators before his assassination in 1678. These copper-plate
engraved cards are much prized by collectors. The earliest ones
date from the Restoration in 1660 and the latest to the 1860's.
Look out also for the 17th century heraldic cards and geographical
cards engraved by Winstanley. 'Aesop's Fables', issued in 1750,
is a series much in demand, as well as 'London Street Cries' with
engravings by Wheatley, issued in 1795; and throughout the 18th
century and well into Queen Victoria's reign educational cards
were made for children.

One pack of Italian Tarot cards, with French names, are decorated on the back with a red pattern of lozenges and stars, which is an unusual feature. At this time backs were generally plain.

Cards were cheap in the early 18th century, unlike those of Tudor times. They were sold in vast quantities for only a few pence. But in 1711 the Lord Chancellor of the day levied a duty of sixpence on each pack, which was a good deal at that period. One can imagine the wrath of the poor cribbage and all-fours men at such an imposition. The tax ranged from sixpence up to two and sixpence until as late as 1862; after that it remained at threepence. The ace of spades was chosen as the receipt for duty paid.

The ace containing the quarterings of George IV, designed in 1828, was known affectionately as 'Old Frizzle' on account of the elaborate twirls and flourishes emblazoned on it. Double-headed court cards and figure indices were not known in this country until the 1860's.

The quality of cards varied. Until the 1790's they were printed on silky 'genoa' paper which took the colour and glaze better than the harsher English paper. Right up until 1832 cards were all hand-made. Inspected carefully for faults, they were classified as Moguls, Harrys and Highlanders according to quality. Then Thomas De La Rue took out a patent for printing the cards by machinery and the hand-made cards gradually died out by the 1850's.

A point which can also help to date the cards is the fact that from 1840 they had glossy surfaces, whereas before this they were mostly plain-backed with a rough surface.

Should you be lucky enough to be in Paris, you could see at the Musée Carnavalet a charming picture of a card factory dated 1680. Strips of 'genoa' paper lie on the floor, where several cats and dogs are sporting together. There is a press at one side, and about eighteen men and women in aprons are cheerfully at work. A buyer in a perriwig watches his pack or 'pair' of cards, as they called them then, being tied up with string by a fashionably dressed lady behind a counter. Two people are vetting the sheets of completed cards.

The elaborate and beautiful Oriental cards are another collector's prize; these were made in many shapes and sizes, including circular and triangular ones, and were often of ivory or bone.

It is tempting to link games boxes with a collection of cards. An Eskimo cribbage board from Alaska in the shape of a lovable seal, for instance is difficult to resist. The elegant Pope Joan gambling wheels are also most decorative, made of painted wood or papier-mâché in most cases. Napoleonic prisoners of war made little card packs out of bone.

The French Duc de Visconti in the fourteenth century, when prices of cards were astronomical, ordered a pack or bunch, as they called them in his day, and paid 1500 écus d'or for them. About 1880 a five of diamonds was discovered from this pack, on the back of which Holbein had painted and signed a miniature in gouache. This was sold for £2,750. What would it fetch now?

As well as standard packs, there were others designed to catch the attention and relay educational lessons, moral precepts, studies of grammar and mathematics, geography, music and religion, to mention but a few. These are not easy quarry to find either, as many were 18th century ones. In England we had cards with propaganda on them in favour of such schemes as populating the Bahamas. A very rare but sought after pack was devoted to the lyrics and music of *The Beggar's Opera*. There are map cards, astronomical cards, even cookery cards of the 18th century. The variety is endless and tempting.

At present children's educational cards of the 19th century are quite easy to find and games of the *Happy Families* type were very popular. An earlier instructive game, found not long ago, is one in which the cards are in pairs. Children had to find the corresponding cards to fit the ones dealt to them and so learnt their multiplication tables very painlessly. The charming little hand-coloured pictures really deserve to be framed. Their date is circa 1840, though 'twice one are two' shows a very old-world pair in which the aged gentleman is dressed in late 18th century clothes and his lady wears a *calèche* bonnet of the same period.

Miniature cards, some about half an inch high, and graduating to the size of pocket patience cards which really can be used for play and not simply looked at with admiration, are seemingly mostly late 19th century and 20th century toys. There must surely have been 18th century ones made to equip the baby houses' card-rooms, but I have never seen any early ones. However, the tiny packs turn up from time to time exquisitely printed and often gilded round the edges and fitted into microscopic boxes.

A side-line of card collecting is the charming mother-of-pearl counters that were used in the 18th and 19th centuries, some being in the form of fishes, like those Jane Austen's Lydia Bennett was so pleased to win. Another form of miniature fish is sometimes confused with the counters. It is generally made of bone and is exactly the same size, but in fact it is a bobbin used in the making of macramé fringes for towels or tablecloths. Mrs. Delany, the friend of Queen Charlotte and George III, mentions that when she was visiting the Court in 1782 the Queen 'was making a fringe, in a frame, and did me the honour to show me how to do it and to say that she thought it was a work that would not try my eyes.'

LOOKING AFTER SOME OF YOUR COLLECTION

Jewellery

The care of jewellery requires eau-de-cologne, methylated spirits, a very soft toothbrush or jewellers' silver brush and a soft polishing cloth. Also, jewellers' rouge or a plate-cleaning powder is necessary and lukewarm soapy water and probably camphorated chalk from the chemist.

Most precious stones thrive on a dip into methylated spirits or eau-de-cologne, with a gentle brush and polish afterwards. The exceptions to this rule are turquoise, opals and pearls. Opals, which are porous and brittle, dislike water or heat; turquoise are best cleaned with either camphorated chalk or powdered magnesia and discoloured pearls can be given this same treatment; afterwards use the soft toothbrush to get rid of surplus powder. Pearls in necklaces can be given a rinse in mild detergent and water or soapy water, but they respond best to being worn as the natural oils of the skin are their finest beauty treatment.

Rings with closed backs are probably concealing cement or glue so refrain from a soaking which might dissolve these substances. Jewellers' rouge on a brush dipped into methylated spirits will clean them and the setting will be safe from harm. Then gently polish with your soft cloth.

Be careful of both sapphires and rubies which are not hard gems. Hot water may crack them. Warm soapy water can be used to clean emeralds, rubies and garnets, but aquamarine stones are delicate too and it is only too easy to crack them.

Diamonds may be given a soaking in gentle detergent and water and then rinsed carefully and dried. Cameos can be wiped with a soapy water cloth wrung out well and then rinsed and dried. Marcasite looks well after a polish with a silver cloth.

Remember that diamonds are so hard that they can scratch

other stones, so wrap each piece of jewellery separately if possible when not in use.

Glass

A cardinal rule is to keep glass dry as it is badly affected by humidity and needs good ventilation. Old glass wrapped up in tissue or other paper and put out of sight and mind in a cupboard is not advisable; the cupboard or the paper might be damp. Glass positively enjoys central heating.

Wash your glass in warm water and a mild detergent, making sure that you clean each piece separately as glass can scratch glass. If you add a little borax to the last rinse it will make the glass sparkle.

Two glasses sometimes get jammed together. Try pouring cold water into the inside glass, and then put the two prisoners into a basin of hot water half way up the outer glass, when they should separate after a few minutes.

Ammonia, vinegar or the old-fashioned method of sand and water or lead-shot in water may help if your glass is suffering from a cloudy stain, which frequently appears in decanters or vases. This has been caused by damp or dregs of wine left in the decanter and has actually damaged the surface of the glass, so any treatment is designed to wear off this damaged part.

Cracks and breakages are not to be tackled by the amateur, if the glass is valuable. Experts can file away chips on the top of wine-glasses or take away the bruises on paperweights caused by a fall.

Sticking of stoppers in decanters or scent bottles have several remedies, one sure if another fails. A mixture of salt and glycerine and alcohol is one method; the Victorians used methylated spirits or cooking oil. Greatly daring you might consider giving a sharp tap to your glass with another pieces of glass.

The remarkable Mrs. Beeton, who died when she was only 28, writes as though she were three times her age. 'Glasses should be dipped in water and wiped immediately,' she orders categorically. 'If turned down and left for a few minutes it will be more difficult to prevent their looking dull and smeared. *Cold* water is quite as good as hot.' As for auctions, where one so often finds exciting treasure-trove, 'Never attend auction rooms,' says Mrs. Beeton:

'in the first place because they are not the place for a lady; and in the second, because, unless endowed with extraordinary (sic) acute perception, you are almost certain to be woefully imposed upon.'

Pests

There are so many of these enemies of antique collectors and one remembers Parson Woodforde's battle with one of the nastiest which mercifully are rare in our enlightened age of good sanitation. He spent a night at an inn when he was 'bit terribly by the Buggs last Night' and came home 'terribly swelled in the face and hands by the Buggs'. The state of the 17th and 18th century wigs is notorious and Pepys frequently notes the sessions with his hairdresser when he went to have the nits removed. Again, Parson Woodforde catalogues the visits of Cobb the Rat-Catcher who disposed of a great number living and multiplying in his barn; and Celia Fiennes, that intrepid lady-traveller of the 17th century hardly ever visited Scotland for fear of the pests in the houses of the great. No wonder pomanders and vinaigrettes and those charming little pastille-burner cottages were so popular. Mrs. Beeton even has a chapter in her monumental work which is headed 'Bedroom Pests'.

The furniture beetle enjoys not only walnut and soft woods, but it feeds with considerable appetite on books and paper. Unfortunately it multiplies with alarming speed and after a tunnelling existence of two years it turns into a pupa and starts the cycle all over again. Inject *every* hole you can see with one of the brands of insecticide like Cuprinol or Rentokil, squirting the liquid from a tube and then repeat this treatment a few weeks later. Fumigation in an enclosed room is an excellent method if you dare try the evil-smelling and inflammable naphthalene or paradichlorbenzene or carbon disulphide. Fill up holes afterwards with sawdust and glue mixed together and then paint with stain.

Clothes moths not only eat every fabric they can get at but also take up residence in old pianos too. Brushing and cleaning textiles is the best preventive and storing afterwards in mothproof bags with crystals of paradichlorbenzene, which any chemist stocks.

Dry rot fungus needs expert help, but miniature and small pieces can be fumigated after the offending pieces have been drastically removed by the carpenter-surgeon's knife. Soak them after treatment in paraffin wax.

The wretched housefly marks and stains furniture and glass and these can be removed by the finest blade of a penknife and I have been told that ink-stain removers will deal with the fly stains.

Books and prints and pictures can be literally eaten up by mildew. Keep them out of dark and damp storage and try a bath of solution of permanganate of potash followed by another soaking in oxalic acid, if you don't mind its being very poisonous and dangerous. The solution should be 5% acid to 95% water. Better perhaps to go to the expert restorer.

Silver fish like a good meal of paper and books. Fumigation is the best answer here.

A threat I had not considered until browsing through an old household book of the last century was the carpet beetle. 'Clean your carpets out of doors and then spray with petrol or benzene. Leave them to dry in the sun. Spray cracks and crevices on the floor with paraffin before re-laying the carpet.'

The cure sounds more dangerous than the disease, Another fire hazard, one might think. Is this worse than the pest?[1]

Fans

To clean the sticks of a fan, methylated spirits on a soft rag cleans bone or ivory; never use water on these, but tortoiseshell can be washed with soap and water. Materials can generally be cleaned with Fullers earth, and paper fans should be given the soft bread-crumb treatment or a good art eraser will do equally well. If you try to mend a tear it is best to use a paste. It is possible to get Japanese paper at most art shops and this is transparent enough to paste it over drawings or designs painted on your fans.

As for repairing the sticks, it is not a job to undertake lightly unless you are a very good handyman. The pieces have to be fitted together like a jigsaw and fixed with some good strong epoxy resin like araldite. It is virtually impossible to replace tortoiseshell or

[1] The re-appearance of this old enemy has recently (October 1971) hit the headlines.

bone or ivory sticks unless you have another old fan, and even then the intricate carving on one may not fit the one you want to mend. Wooden sticks can more easily be copied by a good cabinet-maker. One word of warning; if you are going to repair one of those threaded through with ribbons do not rip out the old ribbon until you have memorised exactly how it was threaded through the sticks.

Metals

Copper and brass are supposed to be very easy to clean, but in fact they bring many problems. In copper and bronze as well as brass the patina is one of their great attractions which cleaning too vigorously may destroy. Jewellers' rouge is preferable to the far quicker method of scratching away with pads of wire wool or household cleaners that are both abrasive and hold bleach.

Brass polish usually takes off tarnish on copper and badly corroded brass may respond to a wash or even a boiling in a solution of water and household soda. All these metals can be lacquered after cleaning.

Ormolu must be very carefully treated or the thin coating of gold may be damaged. You might try a weak solution of ammonia and water to take off the dirt and tarnish. The expert will use cyanide if ammonia fails; but please don't try it yourself.

Bronze has a nasty illness called 'bronze disease' which is apparent from the sickly green spots that very quickly spread. This again needs an expert restorer's care, but meanwhile brush off the offending spots and keep your treasure in a dry place.

Lead does not appreciate scrubbing and rubbing as it is a very soft metal. Tin can be treated to gentle cleaning with jewellers' rouge. Iron and steel unfortunately rust easily and there is a commercial product called 'Plus-gas fluid A' which can be applied, followed by 'Jenolite'. But even so you may find that the enemy rust has bitten deeply into your piece of iron or steel and nothing can be done. Damp is once more the main culprit. Beeswax and turpentine followed by furniture polish may help to protect your antiques from trouble. As always, with valuable treasures, do go to the professional.

Pewter, that beautiful alloy of lead and tin, is extremely soft and so don't try the old-fashioned remedies on the beautiful old patina or its value will be lost as well as its beauty. Go to the professional for advice.

Silver should be treated as the soft and delicate metal that it is and respected by never letting it get scratched, which is a hazard that it very easily suffers from. It hates damp and the best cleaner I know is the long-term Silver Foam by Goddard, or, else the same firm's Silver-Dip, just so long as you do only dip and don't leave the silver in the dip too long; rinse well afterwards before drying and softly rubbing with a cloth to give it a polish.

Bone and Ivory

The chief difference between bone and ivory is that bone is not so hard. The best treatment, if it is in very poor condition, is to saturate it in paraffin wax. Bone, like ivory, had been carved and made into attractive pieces since time immemorial. Some of the most sought-after objects are those ship models, cribbage and domino boxes, chessmen, miniature toys and even clock-cases and frames which were made by the French and Dutch prisoners-of-war[1]. They found the bone they used very conveniently in the prison kitchens.

Bone and ivory can both be mended with Durofix types of synthetic glue, but if either is stained that is quite a problem, as the stain will have penetrated right the way through. If your piece is valuable or if you are fond of it, give it into the hands of a man who knows how to treat it properly. Water and methylated spirits can be tried on less desirable objects, or even a little whiting as finely powdered as possible. See that it is very well dried afterwards and then you might rub it with an oil like almond oil, which is recommended by some dealers. Replacements of any kind are best left to a knowledgeable craftsman.

Sam Beeton, the famous Isabella's husband, has a strange little paragraph on 'How to Silver Ivory'. In case anybody wishes to treat a piece in this peculiar way, here is the recipe: 'Immerse the ivory in a weak solution of nitrate of silver and let it remain until the solution has given it a deep yellow colour: then take it out and immerse it in a tumbler of clear water, exposing it (in the water)

[1] Between 1756 and 1815 we had thousands of these p.o.ws. in our prisons. See *Prisoners-of-War Work* by Jane Toller.

174

to the rays of the sun. In about three hours the ivory assumes a black colour; but this black surface is soon changed to a brilliant silver.' Lastly, remember that very old ivory is inclined to be brittle; and by the way, that beautiful patina of ancient ivory, a lovely rich creamy colour, is most desirable, so hesitate before you take up the bottle of bleach.

Frames, Prints and Books

Russian leather, which is scented with the tar of the beech tree, never gets mouldy. A time-honoured way of combating mould used to be to rub the leather bindings with cedar-oil. Apparently this treatment was known at least as long ago as Horace the Latin poet who was writing about 65 B.C. His expression *digna cedro* is said to mean any work worthy of being anointed with cedar-oil deserved to be preserved and remembered. Nevertheless, the best possible way to look after old books is to read them, air their pages and handle their leather bindings. Central heating, by the way, is one of their worst enemies. For any re-binding or restoration it is best to go to the expert.

Mrs. Rundell, who wrote a book on cooking and housekeeping in 1867, has a recipe for making a 'Liquor to wash Old Deeds, etc. on paper or parchment, when the writing is obliterated, or when sunk, to make it legible.' All you need is 'five or six galls, bruise them and put them with a pint of strong white wine; let it stand in the sun two days. Then dip a brush into the wine and wash the part of the writing which is sunk.' Gall is normally the gall-bladder, perhaps of the chicken; but the recipe I own baffles me. Mrs. Rundell has no solution for preserving the gilding on frames other than the defeatist approach of covering it with strips of paper until the flies, which do most of the damage, have gone to bed for the winter. She does, however, give us the useful tip that we should never use linen to wipe gilding with as it removes the gilt and deadens its brightness.

Another old recipe for cleaning frames was soft-soap—'as much as will be on a shilling'—mixed with $\frac{1}{2}$ pt. of rain water. Shake it up well in a bottle and add $\frac{1}{2}$ wineglassful of spirit of hartshorn. Ammonia, I suppose, would do if you haven't a stag's antler handy. Brush over your frame, using a soft camel-hair paint brush. Leave it on for a few minutes and then rinse in soft rain water. Next day the gilt frame may be lightly rubbed with a wash leather.

Today's hints are less complicated. Use warmed turpentine substitute. If the frame is very dirty, half a raw onion will clean it. Rinse it with clean water and then polish it with a good liquid furniture polish. Vinegar and water is another less malodorous recipe.

Frames of wood need the same care as furniture. Walnut can be given either the raw onion or the vinegar and water treatment. Mahogany and oak like a rub with warm beer or warm tea, minus of course the tea-leaves which may be used to clean your carpet. Afterwards dry the wood and polish it. Chipped frames can be mended by plastic wood and then stained or gilded over the repair. Don't hang pictures above the radiator, by the way, or they may discolour. Nor should they hang over the fireplace, unless they are glazed, and glass on pictures should not be cleaned with water as damp is another danger to pictures.

Good oil paintings should be cleaned by an expert, not by yourself or by the little man round the corner.

Dirt and pencil marks on prints or drawings can either be cleaned with breadcrumbs in the old-fashioned way, or else with the special erasers on the market like Artgum. Don't use indiarubber and NEVER use ordinary household bleach. There is a safe agent called Chloramine T available. Any really valuable prints, drawings or water-colours should, like oil-paintings, get expert handling. When looking after your antiques it is by no means always good advice to do-it-yourself.

BIBLIOGRAPHY

ALBERT, L. S. and KENT, K.: *The Complete Button Book*. 1949
 Art Journal of 1870
BARRINGTON HAYNES, E.: *Glass Through the Ages*. 1948
BEDFORD, John: *The Collecting Man*. 1968
CHARLESTON, R. J.: *English Porcelain*. 1965
COLEMAN: *The Collectors' Encyclopaedia of Dolls*. 1968
CUNNINGHAM, Phyllis and BUCK, Anne: *Children's Costume in England*. 1965
CULFF, Robert: *The World of Toys*. 1969
DELIEB, Eric: *Silver Boxes*. 1968
 Domestic Magazine. 1850+
ELVILLE, E. M.: *The Collectors' Dictionary of Glass*. 1961
GODDEN, G. A. (F.R.S.A.): *Illustrated Encyclopaedia of British Pottery and Porcelain*. 1966
GRÖBER, Karl: *Childrens' Toys of Bygone Days*. 1928
HAGGAR, R. G.: *English Country Pottery*. 1950
HEATH, Dudley: *Miniatures*. 1905
HILLIER, Mary: *Dolls and Doll Makers*. 1968
HUGHES, G. Bernard: *English and Scottish Earthenware*. 1961
 Small Antique Silverware. 1957
LAMBERT, M. and MARX, Enid: *English Popular Art*. 1951
LE CORBEILLER, Clare: *European and American Snuff-Boxes (1730–1830)*. 1966
NATHAN, Fernand: *Histoire de Jeux Educatifs*. 1969
PLOWER, Margaret: *Victorian Jewellery*. 1951
REMISE, J. and FONDIN, J.: *The Golden Age of Toys*. 1967
SAVAGE, George: *The Antique Collectors' Handbook*. 1959
SPIELMANN, P. E.: *Catalogue of the Library of Miniature Books*. 1961
STANLEY, Louis T.: *Collecting Staffordshire Pottery*. 1963
TOLLER, Jane: *Antique Miniature Furniture*. 1966
 Regency and Victorian Crafts. 1969
 Prisoners of War Work. 1965
WILKINSON. O. N.: *Old Glass*. 1968
YARWOOD, Doreen: *English Costume*. 1952